Enragés and Situationists in the Occupation Movement, France, May '68

ABOLITION
DE LA
SOCIÉTÉ
DE
CLASSE

CONSEIL POUR LE MAINTIEN DES OCCUPATIONS

"ABOLISH CLASS SOCIETY!"
Council for the Maintenance of Occupations

Enragés and Situationists in the Occupation Movement, France, May '68

René Viénet

Autonomedia, New York
Rebel Press, London

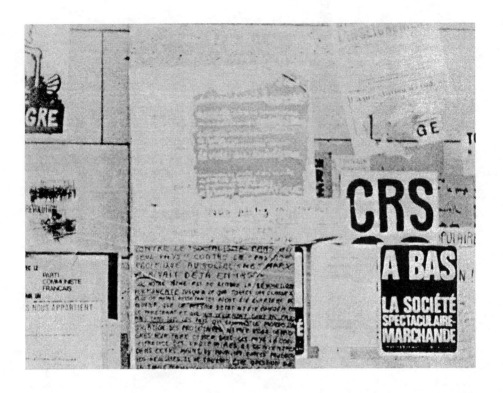

Original edition ©1968 by
Éditions Gallimard
Paris, France.

All rights reserved.
This edition ©1992 by
Autonomedia
POB 568 Williamsburgh Station
Brooklyn, New York 11211-0568 USA
(718) 387-6471

Published in association with Rebel Press
84b Whitechapel High Street
London E1 England

Printed in the United States of America

Contents

Acknowledgements 6

Foreword 7

Abbreviations and References 8

1   The Return of the Social Revolution 11

2   The Origins of the Agitation in France 19

3   The Struggle in the Streets 25

4   The Sorbonne Occupied 43

5   The General Wildcat Strike 61

6   The Depth and Limits
        of the Revolutionary Crisis 71

7   The High Point 91

8   The "Council for the Maintenance of Occupations"
        and Councilist Tendencies 95

9   The State Reestablished 107

10 The Perspective for World Revolution
        after the Occupation Movement 117

Appendix: Documents 123

The Committee for the Maintenance of Occupations, Sorbonne, May 17th.

Acknowledgements

Autonomedia and Rebel Press would like to thank the following individuals
for assistance in the production of this book:
Tad Kepley, typing and proofing;
Richard Parry, translation assistance;
Helene Potter, translation assistance;
Carol Saunders, invaluable assistance;
Tom Ward, editing, typing, inspiration;
Jordan Zinovich, copyediting and proofing.

Foreword

The author of this work does not seek to hide his sympathies. So there may be some value in the assertion that he guarantees, and can prove the accuracy of, all reported facts and especially all quoted documents. However, despite the truth of everything he has written, he does not pretend to adequately encompass the whole of the occupation movement. The time for such work will come. At the moment there is almost no available material concerning the provinces and very little about the factories, even in the region of Paris. On the other hand, even in limiting himself to the aspects of the occupation movement studied here, essential but nonetheless circumscribed, the author could not discuss certain aspects of the event because their divulgence could be used against various persons. Given the moment at which this book is to be published, this will be easily understood. The author had the pleasure of collaborating with several members of the Situationist International, two of whom were former members of the Enragés group. Without them the book would certainly not have been written.

—René Viénet,
Brussels, July 26, 1968

One of many sympathetic allusions to the Paris Commune of March–May 1881.

Abbreviations and References

CAL   Comité d'Action Lycéene: High School Action Committee

CFDT   Confédération Française Démocratique du Travail: second largest union in France

CGT   Confédération Générale du Travail: the Communist Party trades union, the largest union in France

CMDO Comité pour le Maintien des Occupations: see chapter 8

CNPF Confédération Nationale du Patronat Française: National Federation of French Employers

CRS   Compagnies Républicaines de Sécurité: national riot police

FER   Fédération des Étudiants Révolutionnaires: Trotskyists

ICO   *Information et Correspondance Ouvrières:* student-run bulletin of working class news

JCR   Jeunesse Communiste Révolutionnaire: the major Trotskyist bureaucratic group of 'Young Communists'

NMPP Nouvelles Messageries de la Presse Parisienne: monopoly distributors of newspapers

OAS   Organisation de l'Armée Secrète: Extreme right wing paramilitary organization responsible for terrorism at the time of the Algerian War for independence

ORTF Offlce de la Radiodiffusion-Télévision Française: government controlled monopoly of radio and television

PCF   Parti Communiste Française: French Communist Party

PTT   Poste, Télégraphe et Télécommunications: national postal, telegraph and telephone system

RATP   Régie Autonome des Transports Parisiens: Paris bus and underground rail system

SFIO   Section Française de l'Internationale Ouvrière: French Socialist Party
SMIG   Salaire Minimum Intégral Garantie: minimum legal wage
SNCF   Société Nationale de Chemins de Fer Française: national railway system
SNESup Syndicat National de l'Education Supérieure: National Union of Employees
                in Higher Education
UDR   Union pour la Défense de la République: from May 30th onwards, both the
                Gaullist party (formerly UNR – Union pour la Nouvelle République)
                and groups of anti-red 'patriots' formed at de Gaulle's call
UNEF   Union Nationale des Étudiants Français: National Union of French Students

Fouchet Reform   Educational reform introduced by Minister Fouchet in
                1966 for the 'modernization' of French education.
                Followed in 1968 by the Faure Reform
Alain Geismar   Maoist secretary of SNESup
Les Halles   Central warehouse district for food distribution in Paris, 'the belly
                of Paris,' where has stood a massive hole in the ground since the
                urbanists demolished it in 1970
L'Humanité   Communist Party daily newspaper
Nouvel Observateur   Modernist left-wing weekly newspaper
Jacques Sauvageot   Recuperator and bureaucratic boss of UNEF
Georges Seguy   Secretary-general of the CGT and a major Stalinist
Sorbonne   The University of Paris

"Concerning original history... the content of these histories is necessarily limited; their essential material is that which is living in the experience of the historian himself and in the current interests of men; that which is living and contemporary in their milieu.

The author describes that in which he has participated, or at least that which he has lived; relatively short periods, figures of individual men and their deeds... it is not sufficient to have been the contemporary of the events described, or to be well-informed about them. The author must belong to the class and social milieu of the actors he is describing; their opinions, way of thought and culture must be the same as his own. In order to really know phenomena and see them in their real context, one must be placed at the summit — not seeing them from below, through the keyhole of morality or any other wisdom."

— Hegel, *Reason in History*

1

Return of the
Social Revolution

Of course, Situationism isn't the spectre haunting industrial civilization, any more than communism was the specter haunting
Europe in 1848.

—François Chatelet, *Nouvel Observateur,*
January 3, 1968

History offers few examples of a social movement with such a depth of
struggle as that which erupted in France in the spring of 1968. It offers none
which so many commentators said was unforeseeable. Yet this explosion was
one of the most foreseeable of all. The simple fact was that never had the
knowledge and historical consciousness of a society been so mystified.

The situationists, for example, who had denounced and fought the "organization of appearances" of the spectacular stage of commodity society, had
for years very precisely foreseen the explosion and its consequences. The
critical theory elaborated and publicized by the Situationist International
(S.I.) readily affirmed, as the precondition of any revolutionary program, that
the proletariat had not been abolished; that capitalism was continuing to
develop its own alienations; and that this antagonism existed over the entire
surface of the planet, along with the social question posed for over a centu-

11

ry. The S.I. explained the deepening and concentration of alienations by the delay of the revolution. That delay obviously flowed from the international defeat of the proletariat since the Russian counter-revolution, and from the complementary extension of capitalist economic development. The S.I. knew perfectly well, as did so many workers with no means of expressing it, that the emancipation of the workers still clashed everywhere with the bureaucratic organizations which are the workers' *autonomized representations*. The bureaucracy was constituted as a class in Russia and subsequently in other countries, by the seizure of totalitarian state power. Elsewhere a stratum of privileged managers, trade unionists or party leaders in the service of the modern bourgeoisie, whose courtiers they had become, worked to integrate the work force into a rational management of the economy. The situationists asserted that the permanent falsification necessary to the survival of those bureaucratic machines, a falsification directed first and foremost against all revolutionary acts and theories, was the master-key to the general falsification of modern society. They had also recognized and set out to unify the new forms of subversion whose first signs were becoming visible, and which were beginning confusedly to draw the perspective of a total critique from the unified oppressive conditions. Thus the situationists demonstrated the imminence of a new revolutionary departure. For many people these perspectives seemed paradoxical, even demented. Now things have been clarified!

In the present return of the revolution, *history itself* is *the unexpected factor* for the philosophers of the state (which is only natural), and the rabble of the pseudo-critique. It's obvious that analysis attains reality only by taking part in the real movement that suppresses existing conditions. The vacuum organized on this account makes everybody's way of life one which not everyone can decipher. It is in this sense that the *familiar* in alienated life and in the refusal of that life is not necessarily *known*. But for the revolutionary critique nothing was more clear and foreseen than the new era of class struggles ushered in by the occupation movement.[1] The revolutionary critique brings its own theory to the practical movement, is deduced from it and is brought to the coherence which it seeks.

The Stalinists, ideologues of the bureaucratic totalitarian form of exploitation, were reduced in France, as elsewhere, to a purely conservative role. For a long time it had been impossible for them to take power, and the international dislocation of the bureaucratic monolith, which is necessarily their frame of reference, had closed this road to them forever. At the same time, that frame of reference, and the practice it entails, made their return to a purely bourgeois reformist apparatus equally impossible. The Maoist variation, reproducing as illusion the ascendant period of Stalinism by the religious contemplation of a revolutionary orient of fantasy, parroted their translations in a perfect vacuum. The three or four Trotskyist sects fought bitterly amongst themselves for the glory of beginning the revolution of 1917 again, as soon as they had succeeded in reconstituting the appropriate party. These "resuscitated Bolsheviks" were too fanatical about the revolutionary past and its worst errors even to look at modern conditions. Some of them mixed this historical exoticism with the geographic exoticism of a more or less Guevarist revolution of underdevelopment. If any of them picked up a militant from time to time this was in no way the result of the truth of their analyses or actions, but simply of the decomposition of the so-called communist bureaucracies.

As for the modernist pseudo-thinkers of the critique of details, these leftovers of militancy who had established themselves in the so-called Humanities Departments and who were thinking for all the weekly magazines, it's obvious they were incapable of understanding — let alone foreseeing — anything whatsoever, eclectically weighed down as they were with almost every aspect of the old world's camouflages. They found themselves too attached to the bourgeois state, to an exhausted Stalinism, to a revitalized Castro-Bolshevism, to psycho-sociology, and even to their own miserable lives. They respected everything. They lied about everything. And we find them around today, still ready to explain everything to us!

The great majority of the masses mobilized by the revolutionary crisis of May began to understand what they were living, and therefore understood what they had previously been living. And those who were able to develop the clearest consciousness recognized the total theory of the revolution as their own. On the other hand, all the specialists of ideology and of so-called agitational and subversive activism foresaw nothing and understood nothing. In such conditions, what could they arouse but pity? They serenely replayed their usual music amid the ruins of that dead time during which they had been able to think of themselves as the future elite of the revolution. The melody, so long expected to be their baptism, proved only to be their funeral knell.

In fact the reappearance of critical theory and critical action historically constituted an objective unity. The era's new needs created their own theory and theoreticians. The dialogue which began in this way, however limited and alienated by conditions of *separation*, moved towards its conscious subjective organization. And, by the same movement, each one of its critiques began to discover all its tasks. Both of them erupted first as a struggle against the new aspects of exploitation in class society. On the one hand the wildcat strikes of the West and the working-class insurrections of the East inaugurated in practice the struggle against the various bureaucracies. On

the other hand, present revolutionary theory began a critique of the conditions of existence inherent in overdeveloped capitalism: the pseudo-abun-
dance of *commodities* and the reduction of life to a *spectacle*, repressive
urbanism and ideology; always in the service of specialists of domination.
When the Situationist International formulated a coherent theory of this
reality, it also showed the negation of this reality in the combined realization
of art and philosophy in the liberation of everyday life.[2] Thus the theory was
both radically new and took up all the old truth of the provisionally
repressed proletarian movement. The new program rediscovered at a higher
level the project of the abolition of class society, of the accession at last to
conscious history and free construction of life, as well as rediscovering the
form of *workers' councils* as its means.

The new revolutionary development in industrialized countries, which is
at the center of all modern history, can be dated from the workers' uprising
in East Berlin in 1953, opposing the bureaucratic imposture in power with
the demand for a "government of steel workers." The Hungarian Revolution
of 1956 began the realization of the power of the councils, though the country was not sufficiently industrialized and the specific conditions were a
national uprising against impoverishment, a foreign oppressor, and general
terror.

The beginning of the student agitation in Berkeley, in the autumn of
1964, questioned the organization of life in the most developed capitalist
country, beginning with the nature of education, and signalled a revolt
which has since extended to almost all European countries.[3] Nevertheless,
this revolt, however advanced in certain of its main themes, remained partial
insofar as it was limited to the "student scene" (itself the object of rapid
transformation related to the needs of modern capital), in as much as its
recent political consciousness remained very fragmented and weighted down
with various neo-Leninist illusions, often including an imbecilic respect for
the Maoist farce of "cultural revolution." The question of the blacks, the
Vietnamese War, and Cuba occupied a disproportionate and mystifying position in the American students' struggle, which was, for all this, nonetheless
real. This "anti-imperialism," reduced to a merely contemplative applause,
almost always dominated the student movements in Europe. Since the summer of 1967 the West Berlin student movement has taken a violent turn —
demonstrations spread throughout Germany in response to the attempt on
Dutschke's life. The Italians went further, after December 1967, particularly
in Turin, occupying the factories and forcing the closure of the major universities of the country at the beginning of 1968.

The current crisis of bureaucratic power in Czechoslovakia, the only
advanced industrial country ever conquered by Stalinism, is essentially a

question of a hazardous attempt by the ruling class to correct on its own initiative the functioning of its seriously failing economy. It was the pressure of agitation by the students and intelligentsia at the end of 1967 that made the bureaucracy decide to run the risk. The workers' strikes and the first rumblings of demands for direct factory control will henceforth pose the chief danger to a bureaucratic power obliged to feign liberalization.

The bureaucratic appropriation of society is inseparable from a totalitarian possession of the state and the absolute reign of its ideology. The absence of censorship, the guarantee of free expression, and the right of association, pose in the very near future the following alternatives for Czechoslovakia: either a repression revealing the pure sham of these concessions, or else a proletarian assault against the bureaucratic property of the state and the economy, which could be unmasked as soon as the dominant ideology was deprived for any length of time of its ever-present police. The outcome of such a conflict will be of the greatest interest to the Russian bureaucracy, whose survival would be endangered by the victory of the Czech workers.[4]

In March the important movement of Polish students also shook Gomulka's regime – the result of a successful bureaucratic reform after the crisis of 1956 and the crushing of the Hungarian workers. The reprieve won in that [earlier] period is coming to an end, but on this occasion the workers did not join the students, who were crushed in isolation. Only the pseudo-workers, party activists, and police from the militias intervened in the moment of crisis.

In France a decisive threshold has been crossed, in which the movement has rediscovered its deepest goals. The workers of a modern capitalist country returned en masse to radical struggle. Everything is again put in question. The lies of an epoch crumble. Nothing can remain as before. Europe can only leap for joy and cry out: "Well dug, old mole!"

The situationist scandal in Strasbourg in December 1966 had sounded the death knell for student-unionism in France. The local bureau of the UNEF (Union National des Étudiantes Français) had suddenly declared itself in favor of the theses of the S.I., publishing Mustapha Khayati's pamphlet *On Student Poverty*... The method used, the ensuing trials, and the implacable coherence of the analysis all contributed to the great success of this lampoon. We can speak here of the first successful attempt to communicate revolutionary theory to the currents which justify it. Approximately ten translations extended the audience of this text, notably in the USA and in Italy. If its immediate practical impact in France was less strongly felt, this was because the country was not yet involved in the struggles already in motion elsewhere. Nonetheless its arguments were not entirely foreign to the contempt which a faction of French "students" was to express later on, much more accurately than in any other country, for the whole of the student milieu, its rules and shibboleths.

The richness of the revolutionary situation in France, which dealt Stalinism the hardest blow it ever sustained in the West, was expressed in the spontaneous takeover by the workers, in their own right, of a large part of a movement explicitly criticizing hierarchy, commodities, ideology, survival, and spectacle. It is also significant to note that the positions or the phrases of the two books of situationist theory which appeared in the last weeks of 1967[5] were written on the walls of Paris and several provincial cities by the most advanced elements of the May uprising. The greater part of these theses took up the greater part of these walls. As was to be expected, situationist theory has become a practical force taking hold of the masses.

Notes

[1] Philippe Labro, describing the French atmosphere before the crisis in his book *Ce N'est Qu'un Debut* (EPP Denoel), ventures to remark that the situationists thought they were speaking in a vacuum. A brave inversion of the truth. It was, of course, Labro, along with so many others, who thought the situationists were speaking in a vacuum.

[2] The term "situationism," never used by the S.I., which is radically opposed to any doctrinal establishment of an ideology, has been abundantly thrown about by the press, lumped in with the most fantastic definitions: "vanguard of the student movement" (*20 Ans*, June 1968), "technique of intellectual terrorism" (*Journal de Dimanche*, May 19, 1968), and so on. Despite the S.I.'s obvious development of the historical thought issuing from the method of Marx and Hegel, the definition by *Carrefour*, May 8, 1968: "more anarchist than the anarchists, who they find too bureaucratic" is the model of the genre.

[3] It is nevertheless necessary to note the persistence of street struggles by radical Japanese students of the Zengekuren since 1960. Their example has been increasingly cited in France in recent years. The political position of their Revolutionary Communist League, to the left of Trotskyism, and simultaneously opposed to imperialism and bureaucracy, was less well-known than their street-fighting techniques.

[4] Three weeks after this book was turned over to the publisher, the intervention of the Russian army in Czechoslovakia on August 21, demonstrated perfectly that the bureaucracy had to break the movement at any price. All the western "fellow-travellers" of the bureaucracy, with their displays of astonishment and regret, are naturally less lucid than their masters concerning the vital interests of those masters.

[5] *La Societé du Spectacle* by Guy Debord (1971 reprint by Éditions Champ Libre, Paris). English translation (first published by Black and Red, Detroit, and revised

in 1977) now available as *Society of the Spectacle* (Rebel Press/AIM Publications, London, 1987). *Traité de savoir-vivre à l'usage des jeunes générations* by Raoul Vaneigem (Gallimard). Retranslated by Donald Nicholson-Smith in 1983 as *The Revolution of Everyday Life* (Rebel Press/Left Bank Books, London and Seattle, latest reprint 1988). *On the Poverty of Student Life Considered in its Economic, Political, Psychological, Sexual, and particularly Intellectual Aspects, and a Modest Proposal for its Remedy*, by members of the Internationale Situationiste and students of Strasbourg, has been freely translated since 1966. (The current edition by Rebel Press/Dark Star Press, London 1985, includes a postscript added later, taken from the English language edition of Champ Libre, Paris 1972.) See also *The Situationist International Anthology*, edited and translated by Ken Knabb (Bureau of Public Secrets, Berkeley, reprinted 1989).

Enragés in the meeting hall at Nanterre University, February, 1968

"IN NANTERRE"
"Like everywhere else, there are no coincidences.
Probability makes for accomplices, while chance creates meaning.
That's when happiness and misery take shape.
1.) 'Has UNEF already taken a position in favor of the dean?'
2.) ' Love, they talk a lot about it, but don't make enough.'
3.) 'Life is one thing, politics another. We must avoid the scandal
that would come from bad tactics.'
4.) Group: 'Who authorizes you to speak like this?'
Man: 'We do.' Woman: 'As soon as we decide that our desires will be reality.'
"Ideas are getting better. The meaning of words helps. Everything is to be
discussed. Blue will remain grey as long as it isn't re-invented. Make a note of it!!
COMRADES, THE ACTION IS YOURS TO TAKE!"

2

Origin of the Agitation in France

Of course, utopians can also correctly see the situation which they must leave. If they remain mere utopians, it is because they are in a position to see the situation only as a fact, or, at best, as a problem to be resolved, without ever realizing that both the solution and the path leading to the solution are to be found precisely in the problem itself.

Georg Lukacs, *History and Class Consciousness*

The refusal already being affirmed by wide sections of youth in other countries had been taken up in France by only a tiny fringe of advanced groups. No tendency towards economic or even political "crisis" could be observed. The agitation launched at Nanterre by four or five revolutionaries, who would later constitute the Enragés, was to lead in less than five months to the near liquidation of the state. This is certainly food for thought. The profound crisis latent in France exists in all other modern bourgeois societies. What was lacking was consciousness of a real revolutionary perspective and its practical organization. Never did an agitation by so few individuals lead in so short a time to such consequence.

The Gaullist regime in itself had no particular importance in the origin of this crisis. Gaullism is nothing but a bourgeois regime working at the modernization of capitalism, in much the same fashion as Wilson's Labor Party is. Its principle characteristic and success lies in the fact that the opposition in France is even more handicapped than elsewhere in attracting support for a program with precisely the same ends. We must nonetheless note two specific features: the Gaullist accession to power by plots and a military putsch, which marks the regime with a certain contempt for legality, and de Gaulle's personal cultivation of archaic prestige. It's ironic that this kind of prestige, so completely lacking in France for one hundred years, began to reappear only with the recent movement, and precisely by shattering the plaster prestige of Gaullism.

The modernization of the French economy and its adaptation to the Common Market, though undramatic, didn't take place without a certain recession and drop in real salaries through the expediency of Government decrees on social security, with a growth in unemployment, especially for young workers. This was the pretext for the exemplary working class riot in Caen in January, where the workers overstepped trade union demands and looted several stores. In March steel workers of the Garnier factory in Redon were able to bring every factory in the town into their victorious strike, creating their own links independently of the trade unions, and organizing their own self-defense, forcing a CRS (riot police) withdrawal.

The direct repercussions of the Strasbourg affair were first felt at the university dormitories of Jussieu, near Lyon, where, for several weeks during the spring of 1967 the residents ignored every regulation, thus going beyond the academic debate on the reform of anti-sexual statutes. From the beginning of December 1967 the "students" of Nantes went further still. After taking over the local branch of the UNEF, they decided to close the Bureau d'Aide Psychologique Universitaire. They then organized several invasions of the university residence halls: men in the women's dormitories, followed by women in the men's. Finally, in February, they seized the Nantes Rectory and fought the police ferociously. As *Rivarol* wrote on May 3rd, "it has largely been forgotten that, as early as February, the riots at Nantes showed the real face of these 'situationists,' fifteen hundred students under red and black flags, the Hall of Justice occupied..."

The Enragés group was formed during a struggle against police presence in Nanterre. Some plain-clothes policemen had been photographed and on January 26th enlarged reproductions were displayed on posters inside the faculty. This action brought on, at the request of Dean Grappin, the intervention of sixty uniformed men, who were driven off after a brief confrontation. Several hundred leftist militants had joined the original instigators. These included the Enragés as such, along with a dozen or so anarchists. The Enragés were among the least assimilated elements of the university system at that time. Moreover these "campus bums" had found their way to a theoretical agreement with the platform of the Situationist International. They began a systematic assault on the unbearable order of things, beginning with the university.

The environment was particularly revolting. Nanterre was modern in its faculty appointments, exactly as it was modern in its architecture. It was here that the cretins of submissive thought pontificated — the knaves of recuperation, the modernist nullities of social integration, the Lefebvres and Tourraines.[1] The scene was perfect: the urbanism of isolation had grafted a university center onto the high-rise flats and their complementary slums. It was a microcosm of the general conditions of oppression, the spirit of a world without spirit. Thus the program preventing the specialists of illusion from speaking *ex cathedra* and the use of the walls for critical vandalism were to have great effect. This opened the exit from the sterile protest regurgitated for years against the pettiness of the dormitory monitors or the Fouchet reform, made to order for the UNEF and for all those who coveted leadership.

When the Enragés began to interrupt the courses of the sociologists and several others, the UNEF and its leftist infiltrators reacted with indignation. On several occasions they themselves attempted to protect the professors. The anarchists, despite intentions of their own regarding the local UNEF committee, stayed neutral. Among them Daniel Cohn-Bendit, who had already carved out for himself something of a reputation by excusing himself for having insulted a Minister, was threatened with no less than expulsion from the UNEF on a motion by the Trotskyists (known at the time as the CLER but who later became the Federation of Revolutionary Students). Only because Cohn-Bendit, a German national, had been called to appear before the committee on expulsions at the Prefecture (national police headquarters) did the CLER decide to withdraw their motion. The scandals of the Enragés were already finding an echo in a certain political agitation. Their song about Grappin, the infamous "Grappignole," and their first comic-strip poster appeared on the occasion of the "National Day" of university residence occupations, February 14. On every side the tone got higher.

On February 14 the *Nouvel Observateur* wept over Nanterre: "The left has dissolved leaving nothing but the Enragés who include no one but three or four representatives of the Situationist International."

The same day the Enragés issued a tract making clear that they

> had never belonged to the Situationist International and therefore could not claim to represent it in any way. Repression would be child's play if every demonstration that showed the slightest radicalism were the result of a Situationist plot!... [W]e nevertheless

reaffirm our sympathy for the situationist critique. Our accord with
radical theory can be judged by our acts.

On March 22nd the leftist groups invaded the administration building and
held a meeting in the university council room. In the name of the Enragés,
René Riesel immediately demanded the expulsion of two observers from the
administration and of several Stalinists who were present. After spokesmen
for the anarchists, a regular collaborator of Cohn-Bendit's, had asserted that
"the Stalinists who are here this evening are no longer Stalinists," the
Enragés immediately left the meeting in protest against this cowardly illusion. They had, moreover, been accused of wanting to wreck the union
offices. They set about writing their slogans on the walls: "TAKE YOUR DESIRES
FOR REALITY," "BOREDOM IS COUNTER-REVOLUTIONARY," "TRADE UNIONS ARE BROTHELS,"
"NEVER WORK," etc. This ushered in a form of agitation that was to enjoy a
far-reaching success and become one of the original characteristics of the
period of occupations. Thus the gathering of various leftist elements which
would be called in the following weeks "The Movement of the 142" and then
the "March 22nd Movement" began to constitute itself that evening, without
and against the Enragés.

From the beginning, the March 22nd Movement was an eclectic conglom-
erate of individuals who joined it under purely personal auspices. They all
agreed on the fact that it was impossible for them to agree on any theoretical
point and counted on "common action" to overcome this gap. There was
nevertheless a *consensus* on two subjects; one a ridiculous banality, the other
a new demand. The banality was the anti-imperialist "struggle," heritage of
the contemplative period of the leftist groups which was about to end:
Nanterre, that suburban Vietnam, lending its resolute support to insurgent
Bolivia. The novelty was direct democracy in the organization. It is true that
this intention was only partially realized in the March 22nd Movement
because of the double allegiance of most of its members, which problem was
discretely ignored or never considered. There were Maoists, JCRs, anarchists
of all kinds, from the ruins of the "Anarchist Federation" to the activists of
the "Iberian Federation of Libertarian Youth," and up to and including the
comical, or questionable, adherents of the "groups of institutional research"
(FGERI).[2]

Cohn-Bendit himself belonged to the independent and semi-theoretical
anarchist group around the magazine *Noir et Rouge*. Because of this and his
personal qualities, Cohn-Bendit found himself in the most radical tendency
of the March 22nd Movement and more truly revolutionary than the whole
of the movement whose spokesman he was to become, and which he therefore had to tolerate.[3] Cohn-Bendit, insufficiently intelligent, confusedly

informed by various individuals on the theoretical problems of the period, skillful enough to entertain a student audience, frank enough to do the job in the arena of leftist maneuvers, supple enough to work with their spokesmen, was an honest but only a mediocre revolutionary. He knew much less than he should have known and did not make the best of what he knew. Besides, by uncritically accepting the "star" role, exhibiting himself for the mob of reporters from the spectacular media, Cohn-Bendit naturally had to watch his remarks, which always combined lucidity with nonsense, the latter being aggravated by the distortion inherent in that kind of communication. In April he was still declaring to anyone that he was a moderate and in no way an Enragé. That was the time when the press, following a Minister, began to call all the Nanterre rebels "Enragés."

In a few days the March 22nd Movement had in fact achieved its chief success, with a bearing on the larger movement as a whole, and which had no relationship at all with the chatter about the "critical university" pirated from the German and Italian examples which had already revealed its inanity.[4] Whereas all the efforts of the committee on "culture and creativity" had never gone beyond a revolutionary aestheticism which even some meager traces of "situationism" could not make interesting, the simple-minded "anti-imperialist" project of holding a meeting at Nanterre on March 29 pushed Dean Grappin to the first and most consequential of a series of administrative blunders which rapidly extended the agitation. Grappin closed his campus for two days. The menacing specter of a "handful of Enragés" was beginning to haunt the national consciousness.

Among the most concerned, *L'Humanité,* on 29 March denounced

> the commando actions undertaken by a group of anarchists and 'situationists,' one of whose slogans — in giant letters — "DON'T WORK!" — decorated the entrance to the campus. For those forty or so students, activity has consisted for several weeks in 'intervening' in the lecture halls and discussion sections... occupying the buildings and finally covering the walls with gigantic slogans. How has a handful of irresponsible elements been able to provoke such serious decisions, affecting twelve thousand students in the arts and four thousand in law.

The repressions that began at that moment came too late. Of course, one of the Engragés, Gérard Bigorgue, was effectively expelled for five years from all institutions of higher learning in France without a word from the March 22nd Movement, its journalists, or any other leftist groups (he was reproached for his open contempt for university rules, and his attitude in front of the University Council was in fact scandalous). But renewed threats of expulsion against Cohn-Bendit (already fairly famous and certainly more defensible for many people); the announcement that Riesel, Cohn-Bendit and six other agitators from Nanterre were to be brought before the Committee of the Institution of the University of Paris on May 6th; and, finally, the closing until further notice of Nanterre on May 2nd, provoked an expansion of the agitation among Parisian students. The March 22nd Movement and the UNEF called for a meeting in the courtyard of the Sorbonne on Friday, May 3rd. By trying to break up the meeting, the authorities unleashed the accumulated strength of the movement and provoked it to cross the decisive threshold. How impossible such a development appeared to specialized "observers" is perfectly demonstrated by the brilliant prophesy of the ridiculous Escarpit, who wrote in *Le Monde* on May 4th: "Nothing is less revolutionary, nothing more conformist than the pseudo-anger of a window-breaker, even if he dresses his anti-mandarinism in Marxist or situationist language."

Notes

[1] Towards the end of the 1950s Touraine discovered that the proletariat had disappeared. He persisted in July 1968: "I'll say it again: the working class, as a whole, is no longer a fully revolutionary class in France." (Quoted from Labro, *Ce n'est qu'un début.*)

[2] At no time was there a single situationist in this grab-bag, contrary to the lie of Émile Copfermann in his introduction to the collection of ineptitudes published by the March 22nd Movement under the title *Ce n'est qu'un début, continuons le combat* (Éditions Maspero).

[3] Cohn-Bendit, in a number of interviews, multiplied his concessions to Maoism. For example, in *Le Magazine Littéraire* of May 68: "I don't know that much about what Maoism is. I've read things in Mao that are very true. His thesis of reliance upon the peasantry has always been an anarchist thesis."

[4] All the sociological-journalistic eulogies on the "originality" of the March 22nd Movement masked the simple fact that its leftist amalgam, while new in France, was a direct copy of the American SDS (Students for a Democratic Society), itself equally eclectic, "democratic" and frequently infiltrated by various old leftist sects. Georges Steiner in *The Sunday Times* of July 21st, enumerating with perfect incomprehension the theses of the S.I. which he considered to be "probably the most advanced of the radical factions," nonetheless saw that Cohn-Bendit was a "weather-beaten conservative" compared with such "absolutists."

3

The Struggle in the Streets

I know that you count them for nothing because the court is armed: but I beg you to let me say that they should count for a great deal the moment they count themselves for everything. That is the point they have come to: they themselves are beginning to count your armies for nothing, and it's very unfortunate that their strength lies precisely in their imagination. One could truly say that what makes them different from all other forms of power is their ability, having reached a certain point, to do everything of which they believe themselves capable.

—Cardinal de Retz, *Memoires*

In itself the meeting of May 3rd was banal: as usual three or four hundred hangers-on had responded to the call. The few dozen fascists of the "Occident" group counter-demonstrated at the beginning of the afternoon on the Boulevard Saint-Michel. Several Enragés at the Sorbonne called for the organization of self-defense. Furniture had to be broken up as there were no clubs. Rector Roche and his policemen thought this would be sufficient pretext for an attack. The police and the *gendarmerie mobile* invaded the courtyard of the Sorbonne without meeting resistance. The students were encircled. The police then offered them free passage out of the courtyard. The students accepted and the first to leave were in fact allowed to pass. The operation took time and other students began to gather outside in the quarter. The remaining two hundred demonstrators inside the Sorbonne, including all the organizers, were arrested. As the police vans carried them away the Latin Quarter erupted. One of the two vans never reached its destination. Only three policemen guarded the second van. They were beaten up, and several dozen demonstrators escaped.

It was the first time in many years that several thousand students in Paris had fought the police for so long and with such energy. Endless charges, greeted with hails of paving stones, failed to clear the Boulevard Saint-Michel and the adjoining streets until several hours later. Some six hundred people were arrested. The immediate reaction of the Syndicat National de l'Enseignment Supérieur (the National Union of Employees in Higher Education, SNES) and of the UNEF was to call for an unlimited strike in higher education. The stiff prison sentences handed out to the four demon-

strators on May 5th only served to confirm the demonstration that had been called for May 6th to put pressure on the University Council.

Naturally the Stalinists did all they could to break the movement. George Marchais' editorial in *L'Humanité* on May 3rd, which exposed this policy almost at the level of parody, angered the mass of students. From that moment on the Stalinists found themselves denied the floor in all the centers of revolutionary agitation which the students began to create.

The whole of May 6th was marked by demonstrations which turned into riots early in the afternoon. The first barricades were thrown up at the Place Maubert and defended for three hours. At the same time fights with the police were breaking out at the bottom of the Boulevard Saint-Michel, at the Place du Châtelet, and in Les Halles. By the early evening the demonstrators

numbered more than ten thousand and were mainly holding the area around the Place Saint-Germain-des-Prés, where they had been reinforced only after 6 P.M. by the bulk of the march organized by the UNEF at Denfert-Rochereau. On May 8th *Le Monde* wrote:

> What followed surpassed in scope and violence everything that had happened throughout an already astonishing day. It was a kind of street fighting that sometimes reached a frenzy, where every blow delivered was immediately returned, and where ground that had

scarcely been conquered was just as quickly retaken... There were
dramatic and senseless moments which, for the observer, seemed
rife with madness.

And on May 7th *L'Aurore* noted: "Alongside the demonstrators could be seen bands of young hoods (*blousons noirs*) armed with steel bars, who had come in from the outlying areas of Paris to help out the students." The fighting lasted until after midnight, especially at Montparnasse.

For the first time cars were overturned and set afire, paving stones were dug up for the barricades, and stores were looted. The use of subversive slogans, which had begun at Nanterre, had now spread to several parts of Paris. Insofar as the rioters were able to strengthen the barricades, and thus their own capacity for counterattack, the police were forced to abandon direct charges for a position strategy which relied mainly on offensive grenades and tear gas.

May 6th also marked the first intervention of workers, *blousons noirs*, the unemployed, and high school students who that morning had organized important demonstrations. The spontaneity and violence of the riots stood in vivid contrast to the platitudes put forth by their academic initiators as goals and slogans. The very fact that the *blousons noirs* had fought in the streets shouting "The Sorbonne to the students!" marked an end to an entire era. A week later these politicized *blousons noirs* were themselves at the Sorbonne.

The UNEF, which had been denouncing the violence throughout the Monday demonstrations, was obliged to change its rhetoric the following day to avoid being totally discredited, and in order to continue its moderating activity. On the other hand the Stalinists of the CGT, giving up completely, preferred to cut themselves off totally from the students in order to keep their hold on those workers who were still isolated from the fighting. Seguy proclaimed at an evening press conference that there would be "no complacency towards the trouble makers and provocateurs who were denigrating the working class, accusing it of being bought off by the bourgeoisie, and who have the outrageous pretension of trying to inculcate it with revolutionary theory and to lead its struggle. Along with other leftists, certain elements are trying to strip student unionism of its legitimate demands and of its mass democratic nature for the benefit of the UNEF. But they are only acting in the interests of established power..."

It was precisely in this context that Geismar, Sauvageot, and Cohn-Bendit could become the apparent leaders of a leaderless movement. The press, radio, and television, in their search for leaders, found no one besides them. They became the inseparable and photogenic stars of a spectacle hastily pasted over the revolutionary reality. By accepting that role they spoke in the name of a movement they did not understand. Of course, to do this they had to accept the greater part of its revolutionary tendencies as far as they manifested themselves (Cohn-Bendit was able to reflect this radical content somewhat better). But since this holy family of improvised neo-leftism could only be the spectacular deformation of the real movement, it represented its most caricatured image. Their Trinity, endlessly offered through the *mass media*, in fact represented the real *communication* which was being sought and realized in the struggle. This trio of ideological charm of 819 varieties could obviously only say the acceptable — and therefore the deformed and recuperated — tolerated by such a means of transmission. While the real meaning of the moment which had propelled them out of nowhere was purely *unacceptable*.

The Enragé René Riesel (left), and "media spokesman" Daniel Cohn-Bendit (right). [The difference in style, to which Viénet here refers, is here obvious. Editor.]

The demonstration of May 7th was so well controlled the UNEF and its hard-pressed monitors that it limited itself to an interminable promenade along a rambling authorized route: from Denfert to the Étoile, and back. The organizers asked for nothing more than the reopening of the Sorbonne, the withdrawal of the police from the Latin Quarter, and the release of the imprisoned students. They continued to mill around for another two days, during which only minor scuffles took place. But the government was reluctant to fulfill even these modest demands. They promised to reopen the Sorbonne, but Sauvegeot and Geismar, who were already being accused of betrayal by an impatient rank-and-file, were forced to announce that the building would be occupied day and night for a sit-in and "a discussion of the problems of the university." In these circumstances, Minister Peyrefitte maintained the police presence in the Sorbonne while reopening Nanterre as a test to measure the "goodwill" of the students.

On Friday the 10th more than twenty thousand people met once again at Denfert-Rochereau. The same organizers discussed where it would be best to lead the demonstration. After a long debate they decided on the ORTF (radio and television center), but with an initial detour past the Ministry of Justice. Arriving at the Latin Quarter, the demonstrators found all the streets leading to the Seine blocked by the police, which was enough to condemn the absurd itinerary once and for all. They decided to stay in the Latin Quarter until the Sorbonne was returned to them. At about 9 P.M. the first barricades went up spontaneously. Everyone recognized instantly the reality of their desires in that act. Never had the passion for destruction shown itself to be so creative. Everyone ran to the barricades.

The leaders had completely lost control. They had to accept the *fait accompli* while making clumsy attempts to minimize it. They protested that the barricades should be strictly defensive; and that the police should not be provoked! Doubtless the forces of order had committed a bad tactical error by allowing the barricades to go up without immediately risking an attack to tear them down. But the construction of a system of barricades solidly defending an entire quarter was *already* an unforgivable step towards the negation of the state: any form of statist power would be obliged to reconquer the barricaded zone that had escaped its power as quickly as possible, or else dissolve. (It was because of the excess of ideological distortion maintained by their idiotic spokesmen that so many people on the barricades believed that the police would not attack them.)

The barricaded quarter was circumscribed by the Boulevard Saint-Michel to the west and Rue Mouffetard to the east, Rue Claude Bernard to the south and the Place du Panthéon to the north, lines touched upon but not controlled by its defenses. Its principal thoroughfares were Rues Gay-Lussac,

Lhomond, and Tournefor, going northwest and southeast, and Rue d'Ulm going north and south. Rue Pierre Curie and Rue Ursulines-Thuillier were the only communications east and west. The area in the hands of the insurgents had an independent existence from 10 P.M. until just after 2 A.M. Attacked at 2:15 A.M. by forces moving in from all sides, the quarter was able to defend itself for more than three hours, continually losing ground on the western section and holding out until 5:30 A.M. at the approaches to Rue Mouffetard.

Between fifteen hundred and two thousand people remained on the barricades at the moment of attack. Students did not make up even half that

"Liberty is the crime which contains all crimes."
A portrait engraved by the Enragé René Riesel.

number. On hand were large numbers of high school students, *blousons noirs*, and a few hundred workers—and not only *young* workers. This was the elite, this was "the scum" (*pègre*). Many foreigners and women took part in

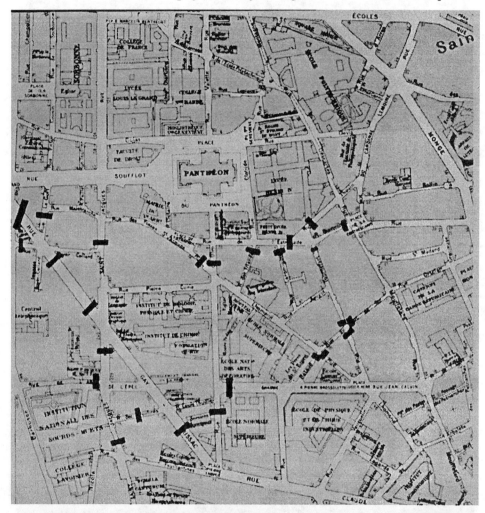

The defense perimeter and the emplacement of principal barricades in the occupied quarter on May 10th.

the fight. The revolutionary elements of almost all the leftist groups were there, notably a large number of anarchists, even some members of the Anarchist Federation — carrying the black flag, which had begun to appear in the street on May 6th, and bitterly defending their stronghold at the intersection of the Rues de l'Estapade, Blainville, and Thouin. The residents of the area showed their sympathy for the very same rioters who were burning their cars by giving them food, water to combat the effects of the gas, and finally refuge from the police.

The sixty barricades, of which twenty were quite solid, allowed a rather

prolonged defense and even some respite from the battle, within a limited perimeter. The weakness of the improvised weapons, and particularly the lack of organization which made it impossible to launch any counterattacks to widen the combat zone, left the rioters caught in a dragnet.

The last pretensions of those who hoped to lead the movement collapsed during the night in shameful resignation and pure impotence. The FER, which had the best disciplined flock, paraded its five hundred militants up to the barricades to declare that the whole affair was the result of provocation and that it was thus necessary to leave. Which they did, red flag leading the way. At the same time, Cohn-Bendit and Sauvegeot, still imprisoned by their obligations as stars, went to tell Rector Roche that "to avoid any bloodshed" the police should be withdrawn from the quarter. This extravagant request, made at such a moment to a man with absolutely no power in the situation, was so surpassed by events that it could only sustain an hour of the most naive illusions. Roche simply advised those who had come to consult with him to tell "the students" to give up and go home.

The battle was very rough. The CRS, the police, and the *gendarmerie mobile* succeeded in making the barricades untenable by an intense bombardment of incendiary, offensive, and chloride gas grenades, before they would risk taking them by assault. The rioters responded with paving stones

and Molotov cocktails. They set fire to cars turned over in zigzag lines of
defense to slow down the enemy advance. Some got onto roofs to drop all
sorts of projectiles onto the police. Several times the police were forced back.
More often the revolutionaries set fire to the barricades they could no longer

hold. There were several hundred injured and five hundred arrests. Four or
five hundred took refuge in the buildings of the École Normale Superieure on
the Rue d'Ulm, which the police did not dare to enter. Two or three hundred
others had been able to pull back to the Rue Monge, or found refuge in the
homes of the residents of the quarter or escaped over the roofs. The police
swept the quarter until noon, beating up and taking off anyone who looked
suspicious.

Notes

[1] Here it is important to point out the gap between the attitude of the organizers and
the real struggle that had been under way for hours: "At the approaches to Place
Denfert-Rochereau, where no police were to be seen... barricades were thrown up
with materials from various construction yards in the area, despite the orders of the
UNEF monitors and several other student organizations." (*Le Monde*, May 8th)

[2] END THE REPRESSION, FREE OUR COMRADES, ROCHE RESIGN, FREEDOM FOR THE TRADE UNIONS,
SORBONNE FOR THE STUDENTS. The same backwardness is to be found in the tone of the
declaration of the national offices of the Fédération des Ètudiants Révolutionnaire
(FER), which on the following day hailed the "thousands of students and young

"I come all over the paving stones!"

workers *who responded to the call of the UNEF to defend democratic and trade union freedom* and who found themselves engaged all Monday with the repressive forces of the Gaullist state." (Author's emphasis.)

[3] The University Council, which was supposed to meet that day to consider the situation at Nanterre, decided to postpone its session because it felt that the necessary calm was not at hand. An anonymous tract, distributed on May 6th, *The Council of the University of Paris: Instruction for its Use*, had revealed the addresses and phone numbers of all its members. The declaration of René Riesel, *The Castle is Burning!*, could therefore not be read by the judges, but was simply distributed to the demonstrators.

Cars burned and stacked like matches. The grafitti, apparently by two sets of hands, reads "Neither God nor Master!" and "Smash the State"

Street scene, the morning after.

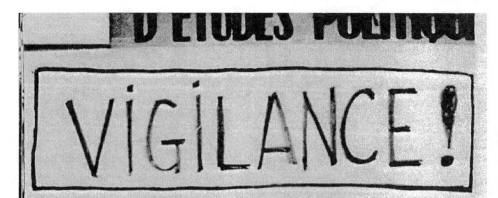

"Vigilance!
The recuperators are among us!
'Annihilate forever all that could one day destroy your work.' — Sade
Enragés — Situationist International"

4

The Sorbonne Occupied

This is where the objective conditions of historical consciousness are reunited. This is where direct active communication is realized, where specialization, hierarchy and separation end, where the existing conditions are transformed into conditions of unity... Only there is the spectacular negation of life negated in its turn. The appearance of the councils was the highest reality of the proletarian movement in the first quarter of this century, a reality which was not seen or was travestied because it disappeared with the rest of the movement which was denied and eliminated by the entire historical experience of the time. In this new moment of proletarian critique, the result returns as the only undefeated point of the defeated movement. The historical consciousness which knows that this is the only milieu where it can exist can now recognize it, no longer at the periphery of what is ebbing, but at the centre of what is rising.

Guy Debord, *The Society of the Spectacle*

The night of the battle around the Rue Gay-Lussac created a stupor throughout the country. For a large part of the population the indignation linked with that stupor was not directed against the rioters, in spite of the extent of the destruction they had caused, but against the excessive violence of the forces of order. The radio had given a minute-by-minute account of the conditions throughout the night, in which the entrenched camp had defended itself and been defeated. It was generally known that a large number of those who had been seriously injured had not received treatment for hours because the besiegers would not let them out. The police also came under fire for the widespread use of a new and ferocious gas, despite earlier denials of its use by the authorities. Finally, it was widely believed that there had been a number of deaths which the police had covered up once they had reconquered the area.[1]

On Saturday May 11th, the whole trade union leadership put out a call for a *one day* general strike on the 13th. For them it was simply a question of putting an end to the movement while getting as much as possible out of the solidarity superficially affirmed "against the repression." The trade unions were also forced to make this gesture because they saw the profound impression that a week of direct struggle had made on the workers. Such an example was in itself a threat to their authority. Their recuperative strike would not respect the time legally required for forewarning; that was to be its sole subversive aspect.

The government, which, in the early morning as the last barricade fell had initially reacted with a threatening statement alluding to a conspiracy and harsh measures, in view of the protest decided on a complete turnabout. Prime Minister Pompidou, who had returned from Afghanistan on Saturday night, quickly dealt the card of appeasement. He announced that the convicted students would be freed immediately after a new trial, thereby overthrowing the hypocrisy concerning the autonomy of the courts. This action was in fact carried out. He allowed the buildings of the Censier annexe of the Faculté des Lettres to be used from Sunday for the legal sit-in that had been demanded for discussion of university reform. The discussion began at once and for several days the studious and moderate atmosphere bore the strain of its birth. Finally, Pompidou promised to withdraw all police from the Latin Quarter on Monday, along with the roadblocks at the entrances to the Sorbonne. On the morning of May 13th the police had decamped and the Sorbonne was there *for the taking.*

Throughout May 13th the call for the strike was widely observed. In an orderly demonstration, nearly one million workers, along with students and professors, crossed Paris from the République to Denfert-Rochereau, meeting with general sympathy along the way. The slogans affirmed the solidarity of workers and students and demanded, on the 10th anniversary of his coming to power, the departure of de Gaulle. More than 100 black flags were scattered through a multitude of red ones, realizing for the first time the union of the two flags which would shortly become the symbol of the most radical current of the occupation movement; not so much the result of an autonomous anarchist presence as an affirmation of worker democracy.

The trade unionists had no trouble getting the crowd to disperse at Denfert. A few thousand demonstrators, mainly students, left for the Champ-de-Mars to hold a meeting. At the same time other students were starting the Sorbonne occupation. There, an event of decisive importance took place: the students present decided to open the Sorbonne to the workers. The abstract slogan of the demonstration —WORKER–STUDENT SOLIDARITY — was taken seriously for the first time. This step had been prepared for by the real encounter

" 'Aaaahhh!!! Situationist International!!! '
Can the pleasures we are permitted compare with those spicier attractions,
those inappreciable pleasures which are connected to the rupture
of social restraints and the throwing out of all laws?"
The first détourned poster, across from the Sorbonne, May 14th.

"Comrades, humanity will only be happy the day when..."

with workers that had taken place that day, and especially by the direct dialogue between the students and advance workers who had come over from the demonstration to say that they had supported the student struggle from the beginning, and to denounce the manipulation of the Stalinists. A certain workerism, cultivated by the bureaucratic specialists of revolution, was certainly bound up in this decision. But what their leaders had said without any conviction and without any real sense of the consequences, took on revolutionary implications because of the atmosphere of *total freedom* that reigned at the Sorbonne, and which completely undermined the implicit paternalism of their plans. In fact, few workers actually came to the Sorbonne. But because the Sorbonne had been declared open to the populace the lines between "the student problem" and a concerned public had been broken. And because the Sorbonne was beginning to have a truly democratic discussion which called everything into question and which sought to implement decisions arrived at collectively, it became a beacon to workers all over the country by showing them their own possibilities.

The complete freedom of expression showed itself in the seizure of the walls as well as in free discussions in all assemblies. The posters of all tendencies, including the Maoists, shared the walls without being torn down or defaced — only the Stalinists of the Communist Party chose to abstain.

Painted inscriptions appeared a little later. That evening the first revolutionary slogan placed in comic strip form on one of the frescos, the famous formula: HUMANITY WILL ONLY BE HAPPY THE DAY THE LAST BUREAUCRAT IS HUNG BY THE GUTS OF THE LAST CAPITALIST. This met with some resistance. After a public debate the majority voted to efface it, which was done.[2]

On May 14th, the Committee of the Enragés and the Situationist International was founded.[3] Its members immediately began putting up posters – which meant what they said – on the walls of the Sorbonne. One warned about the illusions of a direct democracy billeted in the Sorbonne. Another called for vigilance: THE RECUPERATORS ARE AMONGST US! Still another came out against "any survival of art" and the "reign of separation." Finally, one poster called for "the immediate dechristianisation of the Sorbonne," and attacked the blameworthy tolerance shown by the occupiers towards the chapel, which still remained intact. It called for the disinternment and dispatching of the "remains of the foul Richelieu, statesman and cardinal, to the Élysée Palace and the Vatican." It should be noted that this was the first poster in the Sorbonne to be surreptitiously torn down by people who disapproved of its content. The "March 22nd" Culture and Creativity Committee

1) "Those who talk of revolution and class struggle with no explicit reference to daily life, without understanding the subversive character of love and the positive aspects of refusal, have a corpse in their mouth." 2) "Let's de-christianize immediately the Sorbonne. How could one think freely in the shadow of a chapel? Abolish all alienation. Let's exhume nd return to the Vatican and Elysée Palace the remains of Richelieu, statesman and cardinal."

The first copies of a tract by the Commitee for the Maintenance of Occupations
are thrown from the windows of the Jules Bonnot Room at the Sorbonne.

breathed its last on May 14th, with some posters of various quotations by
the S.I., notably from Vaneigem's book.

May 14th also saw the first "general assembly of the occupiers." It proclaimed itself sole power in the Sorbonne and organized the activities of the
occupation. Three tendencies emerged in the debate: a considerable number
of hangers-on, who said little but revealed their moderation by applause for
certain idiotic speeches, simply wanted a university reform, an agreement on
examinations, and a sort of academic front with the left-wing professors. A
stronger current, which brought together the leftist groups and their members, wanted to push the struggle on to the fall of Gaullism or even of capitalism. A third position, put forward by a tiny minority but listened to

ET SI ON BRULAIT
LA SORBONNE?

"And if the Sorbonne burned down?"

nonetheless, demanded the abolition of class society, wage labor, the spectacle, and survival. It was clearly articulated in a declaration by René Riesel in the name of the Enragés. He said that the question of the university had long since been surpassed and that "exams had been cancelled at the barricades." He asked the assembly to come out for the freedom of all rioters, *including those looters* arrested on May 6th. He showed that the only future of the movement was with the workers – not "in their service," but at their side, and that the workers were in no way to be confused with their bureaucratic organizations. He asserted that the present alienation could not be fought while ignoring the alienations of the past – "No more chapels!" – nor those being prepared for tomorrow – "sociologists and psychologists are the new cops." He denounced hierarchical relations with lecturers for being the same kind of policing. He warned of the recuperation of the movement by leftist leaders, and of its foreseeable liquidation by the Stalinists. He concluded with a call for all power to the workers' councils.

There were diverse reactions to his intervention. Riesel's proposal concerning the looters got much more jeering than applause. The attack on the professors shocked the audience, as did the first open attack on the Stalinists. Nonetheless, when the assembly chose the first "Occupation Committee" as its executive organ, Riesel was elected. Alone among the candidates to have indicated his political allegiances, he was also the only one with a stated program. Speaking a second time he made it clear he would defend "direct democracy in the Sorbonne" and the perspective of the international power of workers' councils.

The occupation of the faculties and schools of higher education had begun in Paris – the Beaux-Arts, Nanterre, the Conservatory of Dramatic Arts, Medicine. All the rest would follow.

At the end of the day, May 14th, the workers of the Sud-Aviation plant in Nantes occupied their factory and barricaded themselves in after locking director Duvochel and the managers in the offices and soldering the doors shut. Apart from the example of the Sorbonne, the workers had learned from the incidents which had taken place at Nantes the night before. At the call of the Nantes branch of the UNEF which, as we have seen before, was controlled by revolutionaries, the students refused to limit themselves to a march with the trade unionists. They marched on the police station to demand the end of court proceedings recently begun against them, and the restoration of the annual grant of ten thousand francs which had been taken away after their radical turn. They threw up two barricades which the CRS tried to take back. Some university personnel presented themselves as intermediaries and a truce was made which the prefect of police used to receive a delegation. He gave in on every point. The rector withdrew his complaint to the police and restored the funds. A number of workers from the city had taken part in the fighting and had seen the effectiveness of this type of demand. The workers at Sud-Aviation would remember it next day. The Nantes students immediately offered to support the picket lines.

The occupation of Sud-Aviation, which became generally known on May 15th, was understood by everyone as an act of the greatest importance: if other factories followed the example of that wildcat strike the movement would irreversibly become that historical crisis awaited by the most lucid people. At noon the occupation committee of the Sorbonne sent a telegram of support to the Sud-Aviation strike committee — "From the occupied Sorbonne to occupied Sud-Aviation."

This was the only activity of which the occupation committee was capable for most of the day, and even this was due to Riesel's initiative. In fact, from its first meeting the committee found itself faced with a stupefying contrast between the function delegated to it by the general assembly and the real conditions with which it had to work. The occupation committee was composed of fifteen members, elected and revocable on a daily basis by the general assembly and answerable to it alone. All the services which had been improvised or which remained to be organized for the running and defense of the building were placed under its control. Its responsibilities entailed making possible free discussion on a permanent basis, and assuring and facilitating the extension of the activities already under way, which ranged from the distribution of rooms and food and the democratic diffusion of written and verbal information to the maintenance of security. The reality was quite different: the discredited bureaucrats of the UNEF and the old tandem of Kravetz and Peninou re-emerged from the oblivion which had rightly engulfed them, and slipped into the corridors they knew so well to install themselves in a cellar. From there they prepared to gather up all the reigns of *real power* and to coordinate the actions of all sorts of benevolent technicians who turned out to be their friends. It was a "Coordination Committee" which had elected itself. The "Inter-Faculty Liaison Committee" worked for itself. Its completely autonomous staff obeyed no-one but their leader, a nice guy on the whole, who had appointed himself and was interested in discussion only from that position of strength. The "Press Committee," which was made up of young or future journalists, was not at the disposal of the Sorbonne, but of the French press as a whole. As for the sound equipment, it was quite simply in the hands of right-wing elements who happened to be specialists in electronics.

In this rather surprising situation the occupation committee had some difficulty even in getting a room: each fiefdom that had set itself up had designs on all the offices. A bit discouraged, the majority of the committee's

"Humanity will only be happy the day the last bureaucrat
is hanged with the guts of the last capitalist."

"I take my desires for reality because I believe in the reality of my desires!"

members disappeared and in despair tried to slip into the various floating sub-committees which at least had the merit of existing. It was obvious that the manipulators referred to above had planned to entrench their power by making the elected Committee mere window dressing.[4] They must have been satisfied with the result of their maneuvers on the 15th, because when the general assembly met that evening they proposed to renew *en bloc* the phantom occupation committee for another twenty-four hours. The eight members of the coordination committee were also confirmed as auxiliaries to the occupation committee. Already strengthened by the practical mechanisms at its disposal, the coordination committee planned to round off its seizure of power by telling the occupation committee that it no longer existed. Almost all the members of that committee, who had reappeared just in time to hear themselves re-elected by the general assembly, had resigned themselves to dispersal. Two members alone tried to appeal to the base to denounce the scandalous manner in which the power of the general assembly had been flouted. Riesel spoke to the occupiers in the courtyard, urging them back into the general assembly to repudiate the bureaucrats. Publicly confronted with general indignation, these bureaucrats shamefully withdrew. And what remained of the occupation committee, supported by elements that had suddenly rallied to it, began to exist in reality.

On the same day the workers at the Renault factory at Cléon, in Seine-Maritime, struck and occupied their factory, locking in the management. The Lockheed factory at Beauvais and Unulec in Orléans followed. Later in the evening two to three hundred people arrived at the Odéon Theater as the audience was leaving and took it over. If the content of this "liberation" remained mostly limited — dominated by people and problems of culture —

the very fact of taking over the building completely outside of the university context was nonetheless an extension of the movement, a farcical enactment of the decomposition of the state power. During the night which followed the most beautiful inscriptions of an era appeared on the walls of the Sorbonne.

On the morning of May 16th the occupation of Renault–Cléon became generally known and some of the workers of the Nouvelles Messageries de la Presse Parisienne launched a wildcat strike to prevent the distribution of newspapers. The occupation committee of the Sorbonne, which was meeting in the Jules Bonnot Room (formerly Cavaillès) put out the following statement: "Comrades, the Sud–Aviation factory at Nantes has been occupied for two days by the workers and students of that city. The movement was extended today to several factories (NMPP–Paris, Renault–Cléon, etc). The *Occupation Committee of the Sorbonne* calls for the immediate occupation of all factories in France and the formation of workers' councils. Comrades. reproduce and distribute this appeal as quickly as possible."

As has been shown above, the occupation committee had been stripped of all means at its disposal for the execution of the slightest activity. To distribute its appeal it set out to reappropriate those means. It could count on the support of the Enragés, the situationists and a dozen other revolutionaries. Using a megaphone from the windows of the Jules Bonnot Room they asked for, and received, numerous volunteers from the courtyard. The text was recopied and went to be read in all the other amphitheaters and faculties. Since the printing had been purposely slowed down by the Inter-Faculty Liaison Committee, the Occupation Committee had to requisition machines and organize its own distribution service. Because the sound crew refused to read the text at regular intervals the Occupation Committee had their equip-

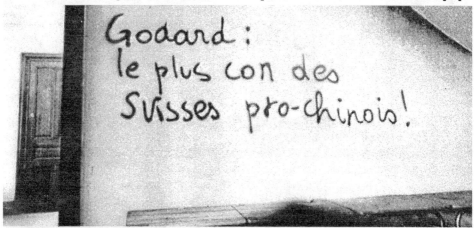

"Godard: the biggest of all the pro-Chinese Swiss assholes!"

ment seized. Out of spite the specialists sabotaged their equipment as they were leaving, and partisans of the committee had to repair it. Telephones were taken over to pass the statement on to press agencies, the provinces, and abroad. By 3:30 P.M. it was beginning to be distributed effectively.

The call for immediate occupation of the factories caused an uproar. Not, of course, among the occupiers of the Sorbonne, where so many came forward to assure its distribution, but among the placement of the small leftist groups who showed up, horrified, to speak of adventurism and madness. They were coldly ignored. The Occupation Committee was not about to be called to account by the various leftist cliques. Thus Krivine, the leader of the JCR, was successfully pushed away from the sound equipment and out of the Jules Bonnot Room, to which he had come running to express his disapproval, his anxiety, and even the ridiculous pretension of cancelling the statement. No matter how much they might have wanted to, the manipulators no longer had the strength to attack the sovereignty of the general assembly with a raid on the Jules Bonnot Room. In fact, since the beginning of the afternoon the Occupation Committee had formed its own security guard since the beginning of the afternoon, to counter any irresponsible use of its shakily established services. It then set about reorganizing these by a discussion with the rank and file, easily persuading them of the anti-demo-

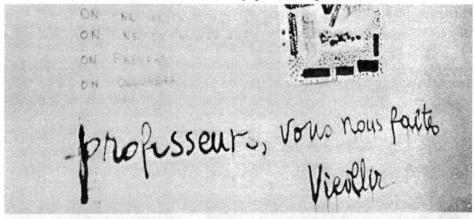

Two sets of grafitti: 1) "We won't ask for anything. We won't demand anything. We'll just take and occupy." 2) "Professors, you make us grow old."

cratic role that certain elements were trying to put over on them.

The task of reconsolidating the Sorbonne was backed up by a series of widely distributed tracts, coming out at an increasing rate. They were also read over the sound system, which was announcing new factory occupations as soon as news arrived. At 4:30 P.M. the tract entitled *Vigilance!* sounded a warning: "The sovereignty of the general assembly has no meaning unless it

"Be cruel!"

exercises its power. For forty-eight hours the carrying out of the general assembly's decisions has been systematically obstructed... The demand for direct democracy is the least support that revolutionary students can offer the revolutionary workers now occupying their factories. It would be unacceptable for the incidents of last night's general assembly to be ignored. The priests are taking over when the anti-clerical posters are torn down..." At 5 P.M. the tract *Watch Out!* denounced the Press Committee which "refuses to transmit the statements of the proceedings regularly voted on by the general assembly" and "which is acting as a *committee of censorship.*" At 6:30 the tract *Watch Out For Manipulators and Bureaucrats!* denounced the uncontrolled monitors. It emphasized the decisive importance of the general assembly which was to meet that evening: "as the workers begin to occupy several factories in France, following *our example and with the same right as us,* the Occupation Committee of the Sorbonne announced its support for the movement at 3 P.M. today. The central problem facing the general assembly is therefore to decide by an unequivocal vote whether to support or disavow the appeal of the Occupation Committee. By disavowing it, this assembly will assume the responsibility of reserving for students a right it refuses to the working class and will make clear that it has no desire to speak of anything but a Gaullist reform of the university." At 7 P.M. a tract proposed a list of radical slogans to be diffused: "POWER TO THE WORKERS' COUNCILS," "DOWN WITH THE SPECTACULAR COMMODITY ECONOMY," "THE END OF THE UNIVERSITY," and so on.

The whole of this activity, which hourly increased the number of supporters of the Occupation Committee, was cynically falsified by the bourgeois press, following *Le Monde* of May 18th, which described it in these terms: "No-one is very sure who is running the Occupation Committee of the Sorbonne. In fact a room where this body, elected every night at 8 P.M., is meeting, was invaded at the end of the afternoon by the Enragés of the Situationist International. In particular they are 'holding' the microphones of the Sorbonne, which allowed them to broadcast several slogans during the night, which many students saw as adventurist: 'IF YOU RUN INTO A COP, SMASH

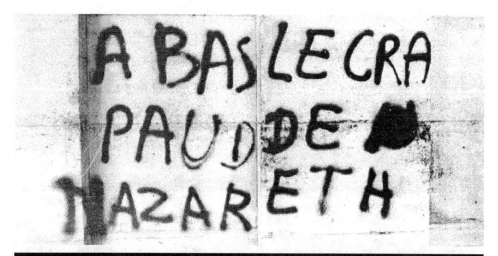

"Down with the toad from Nazareth!"

HIS FACE IN,' 'USE FORCE TO STOP PHOTOGRAPHS BEING TAKEN INSIDE THE SORBONNE.' However the students of the Situationist International have 'dissolved all bureaucratic structures' previously set up, such as the Press Committee and the monitors. The decisions of this committee may be called into question by the general assembly planned to meet this Friday at 2 P.M."[5]

The afternoon of the 16th marked the moment when the working class began to declare its support for the movement in an irreversible way. At 2 P.M. the Renault plant at Flins was occupied. Between 3 P.M. and 5 P.M. a wildcat strike took over Renault–Billancourt. Factory occupations began throughout the provinces. The occupation of public buildings, which continued to spread everywhere, hit Sainte-Anne psychiatric hospital, which was taken over by its personnel.

Confronted by this news, all the leftist groups at the Sorbonne rallied for a march on Billancourt at 8 P.M. The Occupation Committee decided to delay the meeting of the general assembly, which it was nevertheless impatient to confront with its responsibilities. Its statement, issued just before 8 P.M., declared: "In agreement with the different political groups, the March 22nd Movement, and the UNEF, the Occupation Committee has decided to postpone the meeting of the general assembly from 8 P.M. on 16 May to 2 P.M. on the 17th. Everyone meet this evening at 8 P.M. at Place de la Sorbonne, to march on Billancourt."

The entry of Renault–Billancourt into the struggle – the largest factory in France, and one which had so often played a decisive part in social struggles – and particularly the threat of a conjunction of the workers and the revolutionary occupations that had been sparked by the student struggle, horrified both the so-called Communist Party and the government. Even before learning of the plan for a march on Billancourt they reacted almost identically to the bad news they had just received. At 6:30 P.M. a statement from the Stalinist politburo "warned" the workers and students "against all adventurist calls for action." A little later, after 7 P.M., a statement was issued by the government: "In the presence of various attempts called for or set in motion by groups of extremists to provoke general disorder, the Prime Minister wishes to affirm that the government will not tolerate an attack on the Republic... As soon as the university reform is used only as a pretext for plunging the country into chaos, the government has the duty of maintaining public order..." The government at the same time decided to call up ten thousand police reserves.

Some three to four thousand occupiers of the Sorbonne went in two groups to Billancourt under red and black flags. The CGT, which held every entrance to the factory, successfully prevented any contact with the workers. The UNEF and the SNESup were determined to carry out on the following day the plan to march on the ORTF, which the Enragés–Situationist International Committee had been trying to get adopted by the general assembly since May 14th. When this decision became known the CGT declared at 9 A.M. on the 16th that it "looked like a provocation which could only serve personal power." At 10:30 the Stalinist party took the same line. At midnight the SNESup and the UNEF yielded and announced the plan had been cancelled.

During the night the counter-offensive of the manipulators began at the Sorbonne. Taking advantage of the absence of the revolutionary elements who were out at the Renault factory, they tried to improvise a general assembly with those students who had stayed behind. The Occupation Committee sent in two delegates who denounced the character of an assembly growing out of a thin, specious maneuver. Understanding that it had been fooled, the assembly broke up immediately.

At dawn the workers of the NMPP asked the Sorbonne occupiers to reinforce their picket lines, which had not yet succeeded in imposing a work stoppage. The Occupation Committee sent volunteers. On the number two line of the Metro an anti-union action committee attempted to begin a strike throughout the RATP. More than one hundred factories were to be occupied during the day. Early in the morning the workers from the striking Parisian factories, beginning with Renault, began arriving at the Sorbonne to establish the contact which the trades unions were preventing at the factory gates.

The general assembly of 2 P.M. gave priority to a second march on Billancourt, and postponed discussion of all other questions until the evening session. The FER vainly attempted to invade the stage and its leaders spoke just as vainly to prevent the second march, or, if it had to take place, to have it adopt the quasi-Stalinist slogan "ONE WORKERS' FRONT." The FER doubtless saw itself at the head of such a front, along with the SFIO and the CP. Throughout the crisis the FER was to the Stalinist party what the Stalinists were to Gaullism — support triumphed over apparent rivalry and the same services rendered earned, at their respective levels, the same wage of ingratitude. A statement from CGT–Renault had just appeared "actively discouraging the initiators of this march from maintaining that initiative." The march took place. It was received in the same way as the night before. The CGT had discredited itself even more among the workers by posting the following ridiculous calumny both inside and outside the factory: "Young workers/revolutionary elements are trying to arouse division in our ranks and weaken us. These elements are nothing but the henchmen of the bourgeoisie who are receiving large sums from the management."

At 1 P.M. the Occupation Committee had printed a tract by workers who had started the strike at Renault, which explained how young workers had won over the rank-and-file in various sections, forcing the unions to belatedly endorse the movement they had tried to prevent: "Every night the workers are expecting people to come to the gates to give mass support to a mass movement." At the same time telegrams were sent to several countries, expressing the revolutionary position of the occupied Sorbonne.

When the general assembly finally met at 8 P.M. the conditions which had plagued its functioning from the beginning had not improved. The sound equipment worked only for the time necessary for certain announcements and stopped in the middle of others. The direction of the debates, and especially the final vote, were technically dependent on the unknown buffoon, obviously a UNEF hatchet-man, who had appointed himself president of the general assembly at the beginning of the occupation and who, oblivious to all the denunciations and humiliations heaped upon him, clung to this post until the end. The FER, which since that morning had naively publicized its intention to "take charge" of the movement, tried once again to take over the stage. Manipulators from all the sects cooperated to prevent the general assembly from making any pronouncements on the activities of the Occupation Committee which had just asked for a mandate, principally on the call to occupy the factories. This obstruction was accompanied by a campaign of denunciation introducing a number of red herrings: "The Saint Germain-des-Prés appearance" of disorder in the building, the contempt shown for the small leftist groups and the UNEF, the commentary on the occupation of Sainte-Anne in which certain people claimed to have heard a call for the "liberation of the insane," and other miserable topics. The assembly showed itself incapable of self-respect. The ex-Occupation Committee, unable to get a vote on its activities, and having no desire to take part in the power struggles and compromises going on in the various wings around the selection of a new committee, announced that it was leaving the Sorbonne, where direct democracy was being strangled by the bureaucrats. All its supporters left at the same time and the body of monitors found itself dissolved, while the FER, which had been threatening the tribune for more than an hour, seized the occasion to rush in. It was nevertheless unable to take control of the Sorbonne, where the pockets of power were to persist to the end. The verdict of the Occupation Committee was, unfortunately, completely confirmed by the facts.

This collapse of an attempt at direct democracy at the Sorbonne was a defeat for the rest of the occupation movement, which was to experience its main failure precisely in this area. However, at this point of the crisis it is certain that no group had sufficient strength to intervene in a revolutionary direction with any effect. All the organizations that played any effective role in the further developments were enemies of working-class autonomy. Everything was to hang on the power relations in the factories between the workers, everywhere isolated and cut-off, and the joint power of the state and the trade unions.

Notes

[1] This has not been shown to be true. The hypothesis is supported by two considerations: on the one hand it is unlikely that nobody died among so many injured and belatedly treated people; on the other hand it is unlikely that the government would have resigned itself to the considerable retreat, so full of risks, that it was to undertake that very evening without taking into account specific information on the seriousness of the confrontation. There is no question that a modern state has at its disposal the means to cover up a handful of deaths. Not, of course, by counting them as "missing persons" but, as some have argued for example, by presenting them as victims of car smashes outside Paris.

[2] The author of this work is proud to have written this inscription, controversial at the time, but which opened the way to such fertile activity. (See, on this subject, the magazine *International Situationist* no. 11, page 32 onwards.)

[3] Contact between the S.I. and the Enragés had begun on the day after the Enragés' tract appeared, February 21st. Having proved their autonomy, the Enragés could collaborate with the S.I. which had always made such an autonomy the prerequisite of any working relationship. At the end of the occupations the committee agreed to pursue this collaboration with the S.I.

[4] Some time later an exasperated Peninou spared no agony in wailing his complaints to onlookers: "We had all agreed," he moaned, "that no group should participate in the Occupation Committee. We had the agreement of the FER, the JCR, the Maoists, etc. But we had forgotten the situationists!"

[5] These calumnies had a hard time of it. In the *Paris-Match* of July 6th one could read: "This poetic anarchy did not last. A group called 'the Situationists–Enragés' took power by what might be called a 'sectarian legality,' and also took over its essential, necessary, and sufficient instrument, the sound equipment, a system of loudspeakers through which they were able to pour a torrent of slogans into the corridors and courtyard day and night. Whoever has the sound equipment has the floor and the power. The situationists used the equipment to distribute perfectly ludicrous slogans. For example, they called on all students to 'support the patients of Sainte-Anne in their liberation struggle against the psychiatrists.'" In quite another genre, the book by the fascist François Duprat, *Les Journées de mai '68* (Nouvelles Éditions Latines) denounced "40-odd students belonging to the Situationist International" as the instigators of the agitation carried on at Nanterre, and claimed to see the hand of the HVA (the East German Secret Police) in the activities of the S.I. He went on to lump the situationists with the March 22nd Movement and to name Cohn-Bendit as their "old friend."

"Those who go halfway down the path of revolution dig their own graves."
"How can one think freely in the shadow of a chapel?"

5

The General Wildcat Strike

> In France it suffices to be something
> in order to want to be everything.
>
> Karl Marx, *Contribution to the*
> *Critique of Hegel's Philosophy of Right*

During the day of May 17th, the strike extended to almost the entire chemical and metallurgical industries. Following the example of Renault, the workers of Berliet, Rhodiaceta, Rhône–Poulenc and SNECMA decided to occupy their factories. Several railway stations were in the hands of their workers and only a few trains still ran. The postal workers had already taken over the post offices. On the 18th the strike hit Air France and the RATP. Having begun with some exemplary occupations in the provinces, the strike had extended to the Parisian region and then engulfed the entire country. From this moment on even the unions could no longer fool themselves that this chain-reaction of wildcats would not become a general strike.

Spontaneously set in motion, the occupation movement had fought from the beginning all orders and control from the unions. "At Renault headquarters," wrote *Le Monde* on May 18th, "the wildcat nature of the beginning of the movement was underlined after the May 13th strike, which had been moderately supported in the provinces. It was seen as equally paradoxical that the center of the revolt was located precisely in a factory where, at the social level, there had been only routine and minor conflicts."

The depth of the strike limited the unions to a rapid counter-offensive which showed with a particularly brutal clarity their natural function as guardians of capitalist order in the factories. The trade-union strategy had a

The first cartoon produced by the Council for the Maintenance of Occupations. 1. 'All power to the Workers' Councils! Unions are nothing but a tool for integrating into capitalist society.' Signed, Workers on strike 2. 'Something has changed, Mr. President!.' 'Yes! The workers want to run their own affairs!' 3. 'The best thing we can do is get out of here!'

single goal: to defeat the strike. In order to do this the unions, with a long strike-breaking tradition, set out to reduce a vast general strike to a series of isolated strikes at the individual enterprise level. The CGT led the counter-offensive. Beginning on May 17th, its Central Council met and declared: "The action undertaken *on the initiative of the CGT and with the other trade-union organizations* has created a new situation and has taken on an exceptional importance." (This incredible lie is emphasized by the author.) The strike was thus accepted, but only to refuse any call for a general strike. Nevertheless, the workers everywhere voted for an unlimited strike and occupation of the factories. In order to take over a movement that threatened them directly the bureaucratic organizations had first to curb the workers' initiatives and face the growing autonomy of the proletariat. They therefore took over the strike committees, which immediately became veritable police powers charged with *isolating* the workers within the factories and formulating their own demands in the name of the workers.

While the picket lines at virtually all the factory gates, still under union orders, prevented the workers from speaking for themselves or to anyone else, and from hearing about the most radical currents then coming to the fore, the union leadership assumed the task of reducing the entire movement to a program of strictly professional demands. The spectacle of bureaucratic opposition reached the point of parody when the newly de-Christianized

"OCCUPY THE FACTORIES"
Council for the Maintenance of Occupations

Un spectre hante la planète:
le spectre des travailleurs de Sud-Aviation
toutes les vieilles puissances de la terre se sont groupées
en une organisation des nations unies pour traquer ce
spectre: le pape et le president du soviet supreme ,Wilson
et Mitterand,les radicaux de france et les policiers
américains.
Il en resulte un double enseignement:
1°déjà les travailleurs de Sud-Aviation sont reconnus
comme une puissance par toutes les puissances de la planete;
2°il est grand temps que les travailleurs de Sud-Aviation
exposent à la face du monde entier leurs conceptions,
leurs buts et leurs tendances.

"A spectre is haunting the planet: the spectre of Sud-Aviation workers. All the old powers — the Pope, the President of the Supreme Soviet, Wilson and Mitterand, the French Radical Party and the American cops — have united to track the spectre down. The resulting lesson is two-fold: 1) The workers of S–A are thereby recognized as a power by all the rest; 2) It's time for S–A workers to give the world their ideas, goals and political flavor."
A flyer made by the workers of the Sud–Aviation factory in Courbevoie.

CFDT attacked the CGT, which it rightly accused of limiting itself to "subsistence demands," and proclaimed that "...beyond mere material demands it is the problem of management and control of the enterprise which has been posed." This electoral bid by a modernist trade union went so far as to propose "self-management" as the form of "workers' power in the enterprise." This was followed by the spectacle of the two major guardians of false consciousness taking over the truth of their own lies: Seguy, the Stalinist, attacking self-management as an "empty formula" and Descamps, the priest, emptying it of its real content. In fact this quarrel of the ancients and the moderns over the best form of defense for bureaucratic capitalism was only a prelude to their fundamental agreement on the necessity for negotiations with the state and management.

On Monday, May 20th, the strike and occupations became general, with the exception of just a few sectors which would shortly join the movement.

LE POUVOIR AUX CONSEILS DE TRAVAILLEURS

CONSEIL POUR LE MAINTIEN DES OCCUPATIONS

"ALL POWER TO THE WORKERS' COUNCILS!"
Council for the Maintenance of Occupations

There were by now six million strikers. There would be ten million in the days to follow. The CGT and the Communist Party, outflanked on every side, denounced any idea of an "insurrectionary strike," while pretending to stiffen their demands. Seguy declared that his "dossiers were ready for eventual negotiations." For the unions the only use of all the revolutionary strength of the proletariat was to make themselves presentable in the eyes of an effectively dispossessed management and practically nonexistent government.

The same comedy was being played out at the political level. On May 22nd, the motion of censure was defeated amidst general indifference. There was more going on in the factories and streets than in all the meetings of parliament and the parties. The CGT called for a "day of demands" on Friday the 24th. But in the meantime the attempt to expel Cohn-Bendit from the country brought the struggle back into the streets. A protest demonstration was improvised to prepare for the one on Friday. The CGT parade, which began at 2 P.M., was concluded in calm by a particularly senile broadcast by de Gaulle.

Nonetheless, at the same time, thousands of demonstrators had decided once again to defy both the police and the student stewards. The massive participation of workers in the demonstration condemned by the CP and the CGT showed to what extent those two organizations could offer only the spectacle of a strength which no longer belonged to them. In the same way the leader of the March 22nd Movement was able, by his enforced absence, to start an agitation that he would have been unable to restrain.

Some thirty thousand demonstrators had gathered between Gare de Lyon and the Bastille. They set off to march to the Hôtel de Ville. But the police, obviously, had already blocked off all exits. The first barricades went up immediately. It was the signal for a series of confrontations that went on until dawn. Some of the demonstrators were able to break through to the stock exchange and sack it. The fire, which would have fulfilled the dreams of generations of revolutionaries, did only superficial damage to the "Temple of Capital." Several groups had spread out into the areas around the stock exchange, Les Halles and the Bastille, and were moving out towards La Nation. Others had made it to the Left Bank and were holding the Latin Quarter and Saint-Germain-des-Prés, before moving in the direction of Denfert-Rochereau. The violence reached its peak.[1] It had long since ceased to be the monopoly of the "students" and had become the privilege of the proletariat. The police stations at Odéon and in the Rue Beaubourg were enthusiastically sacked. Before the eyes of the impotent police, two paddy-wagons and a police car were fired with Molotov cocktails in front of the Panthéon police station.

At the same time several thousand rioters in Lyon were fighting the police, crushing one superintendent under a runaway truck loaded with stones, and surpassing their Parisian comrades by organizing the looting of a department store. There were battles at Bordeaux, where the police retreated, in Nantes, and even in Strasbourg.

Thus the workers entered the struggle, not only against their unions, but moreover in sympathy with the movement of the students, and better still, of thugs and vandals defending absolutely scandalous slogans, ranging from "I COME OVER THE PAVING STONES" ("*Je jouis dans les paves*") to "NEVER WORK." None of the workers who left the factories to find the revolutionaries and work out a basis of agreement with them ever expressed any reservations about this extreme aspect of the movement. Quite the contrary: the workers didn't hesitate to build barricades, sack police stations, burn cars, and turn the Boulevard Saint-Michel into a vast garden, side-by-side with those Fouchet and the so-called Communist Party would the following day call "scum."

On the 25th the government and the bureaucratic organizations made a joint response to this insurrectionary prelude which made them tremble. Their responses were complementary: both of them called for a ban on demonstrations and for immediate negotiations. Each of them made the decision that the other had hoped for.

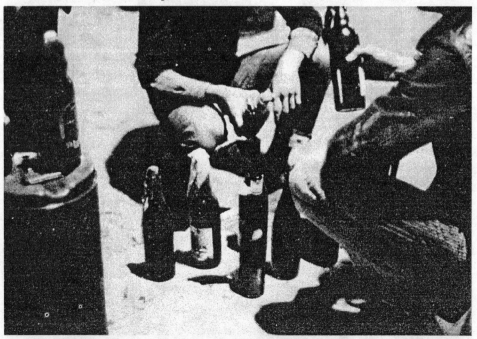

Molotov cocktails.

Note

[1] The death of one of the demonstrators was later admitted. Much use was made of the unfortunate victim: first it was announced that she had fallen from a roof, then that she had been knifed while fighting against "the scum" in the demonstration. Finally, the report of a medical expert, which was divulged a few weeks later, concluded that she had been killed by the explosion of a police grenade.

Police vans and cars on fire outside a police station.

6

Depth and Limits of the Revolutionary Crisis

It was a festival without beginning or end; I saw everyone and no-one, for each individual was lost in the same enormous strolling crowd; I spoke to everyone without remembering either my own words or those spoken by others, because everyone's attention was absorbed at every step by new objects and events, and by unexpected news.

Bakunin, *Confessions*

The occupation movement, which had taken over the key sectors of the economy, very rapidly reached every sector of social life, attacking all the control points of capitalism and bureaucracy. The fact that the strike had now extended to activities which had always escaped subversion in the past radically affirmed two of the oldest assertions of the situationist analysis: that the increasing modernization of capitalism entails the proletarianization of an ever-widening portion of the population; and that as the world of commodities extends its power to all aspects of life, it produces everywhere an extension and deepening of the forces that negate it.

The violence of the negative was such that it not only brought the reserves into battle, side-by-side with the shock troops, but it also allowed the rabble, whose task it was to reinforce the positivity of the dominant world, to permit themselves a kind of opposition. Thus the parallel development of real struggles and their caricature was seen at every level and every moment. The action unleashed by the students in the universities and the streets was extended from the start to the high schools. Despite some student-unionist illusions in the High School Action Committees (Comités d'Action Lycéens — CAL), the high school students proved by their combativeness and their consciousness that they presaged not so much a future generation of students as the grave diggers of the university. Far more than the university professors, the high-school teachers knew how to learn from their students. They overwhelmingly supported the strike, despite the very firm position taken by the school officials. By occupying their workplaces, the employees of banks, insurance companies and department stores had simultaneously protested against their proletarian condition and against a system of services which makes everyone serve the system. In the same way, the strikers of the ORTF, despite a belief in "objective news," had confusedly seen through their reification and grasped the fundamentally falsified character of all communication in which hierarchy is present. The wave of solidarity which carried the enthusiasm of the exploited knew no bounds. The students at the Conservatory of Dramatic Arts took over the buildings and participated massively in the most dynamic phases of the movement. Those from the Conservatory of Music issued a tract calling for a "wild and ephemeral" music and announced that "our demands be accepted within a given time or revolution will follow." They rediscovered the *Congolese tone* that the Lumumbists and Muletists had popularized at the very moment when the working classes of the industrialized countries were beginning to experiment with the possibilities of their own independence, and which expresses so well what all power fears — the naive spontaneity of people awakening to political consciousness. In the same way, the slogan "WE ARE ALL GERMAN JEWS," ridiculous in itself, took on a truly disturbing resonance in the mouths of the Arabs at the Bastille, who were chanting it on the 24th, because every one of them was thinking that it would be necessary to avenge the massacre of October 1961, and that no diversion on the theme of the Arab–Israeli War would prevent it.

Although little came of it, the seizure of the ocean liner *France* by its crew, outside Le Havre, had the merit of reminding those who were now considering the chances of a revolution that the gestures of the sailors of Odessa, Krondstadt and Keil did not belong to the past. The uncommon became the everyday to the extent that everyday life was opening up to astonishing possibilities of change. The researchers of the Meudon Observatory placed astronomical observation under self-management. The national presses were on strike. The grave diggers occupied the cemeteries. The soccer players kicked out the managers from their federation and drafted

"Consume more and live less!"

a tract calling for "soccer to the soccer players." The "old mole" spared nothing — neither the old privileged groups nor the new ones. The interns and young doctors had liquidated the fiefdom which reigned in their profession, spat on the directors before kicking them out, declared their opposition to L'Ordre des Médecins [the French AMA] and put the old conceptions of medicine on trial. The "oppositional managers" went so far as to question their own right to authority, the negative privilege of consuming more and therefore living less. Even the ad-men followed the example of the proletari-

"Either you take over the factories, the offices, the banks and all means of production or you'll disappear without a trace! the revolution needs money and so do you. That's what the banks are here for. Yes to organizing! No to party authority! — Bonnot and Clyde"

"This is the first insurrection in our revolution. 'The true vacation was when we could watch parades for free, when we could light a big fire in the middle of the street and not have the cops show up.' — Harpo Marx (Harpo Speaks)"

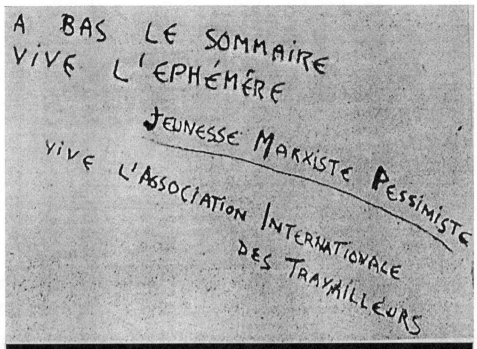

"Beneath the abstract lives the ephemeral!"
Marxist-Pessimist Youth
"Long live the international association of workers!"

ans demanding the end of the proletariat, by demanding an end to advertising.

This clearly manifested will for a real change cast all the more light on the ludicrous and disgusting maneuvers of the falsifiers, of those who make a living by dressing up the old world in new clothes. If the priests were able to get away without having their churches collapse on their heads it was only because revolutionary spontaneity – which in Spain in 1936 had known how to make proper use of religious buildings – still submitted to the yoke of Stalino–Guevarism. Because of that it was no surprise to see the synagogues, temples and churches converted to "opposition centers" to serve up the old mystifications with today's flavorings, with the blessing of those who have been dishing out modernist soup for half a century. Since people were tolerating occupied consistories and Leninist theologians, it became difficult to suffocate in their own smugness museum directors calling for the reform of their warehouses, writers reserving the Hôtel de Massa (which had seen writers before) for the scavengers of the cultural elite, film makers recuperating on film what insurrectionary violence didn't have time to destroy and, finally, artists resurrecting the old sacrament of "revolutionary art."

The police commissariat on the rue Beaubourg on the morning after May 24th.

Nonetheless, in the space of a week millions of people had cast off the weight of alienating conditions, the routine of survival, ideological falsifications, and the inverted world of the spectacle. For the first time since the Commune of 1871, and with a far more promising future, the real individual was absorbing the abstract citizen into his life, his work, and his individual relationships, becoming a "species-being" and thereby recognizing his own powers as social powers. The festival finally gave true holidays to people who had known only work days and leaves of absence. The hierarchical pyramid had melted like a lump of sugar in the May sun. People conversed and were understood in half a word. There were no more intellectuals or workers, but simply revolutionaries engaged in dialogue, generalizing a communication from which only "proletarian" intellectuals and other candidates for leadership felt themselves excluded. In this context the word "comrade" regained its authentic meaning, truly marking the end of separations. And those who used it in the Stalinist sense quickly understood that to speak the language of wolves exposed them as no better than watchdogs. The streets belonged to those who were digging them up.

Everyday life, suddenly rediscovered, became the center of all possible conquests. People who had always worked in the now-occupied offices declared that they could no longer live as before, not even a little better than before. It was obvious in the dawning revolution that from then on there could be no more renunciations, only tactical retreats. When the Odéon was occupied the administrative director withdrew to the back of the stage. After the initial surprise he took a few steps forward and cried out: "Now that you've taken it, keep it, never give it back, burn it first!" And the fact that the Odéon, momentarily in the hands of its cultural galley slaves, did not burn only shows that we have just tasted the first fruits.

Capitalized time stopped. Without any trains, métro, cars, or work the strikers recaptured the time so sadly lost in factories, on motorways, in front of the TV. People strolled, dreamed, learned how to live. Desires began to become, little by little, reality. For the first time youth really existed. Not the social category invented for the needs of the commodity economy by sociologists and economists, but the only real youth, of life lived without dead time, which rejects for the sake of intensity a repressive reference to age. "LONG LIVE THE EPHEMERAL! – MARXIST–PESSIMIST YOUTH" read one inscription. Radical theory, reputed to be so difficult by the intellectuals who were unable to live it, became tangible for all those who felt it in their slightest gestures of refusal, which is why they had no trouble exposing on the walls the theoretical formulations of what they desired to live. One night on the barricades was all that the *blousons noirs* needed to become politicized and reach perfect agreement with the most advanced faction of the occupation movement.

The technical aid of the occupied printing presses was combined with the objective conditions which were foreseen by the S.I., and naturally reinforced the propagation of the situationist theses. Certain printers were among the rare strikers' who, superseding the sterile stage of passive occupation, decided to give practical support to those doing the fighting. Tracts and posters calling for the formation of Workers' Councils thus went through numerous printings. The printers' action followed a clear awareness of the need facing the movement to put instruments of production and centers of consumption at the service of all the strikers, but also arose from a class solidarity that took an exemplary form among other workers. The personnel of the Schlumberger factory explicitly stated that its demands "had nothing to do with wages," and went on to strike in support of the particularly badly exploited workers at the nearby Danone factory. The employees of the FNAC similarly declared in a tract that "We, the workers of the FNAC stores, have gone on strike not for the satisfaction of our particular demands but to participate in a movement which has currently mobilized ten million intellectual and manual workers..."

The reflex of internationalism, which the specialists of peaceful coexistence and the exotic guerrillas had prematurely buried in oblivion or in funeral orations for the stupid Régis Debray, reappeared with a strength which might well augur the impending return of the International Brigades. At the same time, the whole spectacle of foreign policy, with Vietnam in the lead, had suddenly dissolved, revealing itself for what it always was: problems for false oppositions. There was applause for the seizure of Bumidom by the Antillais, the occupations of the international dormitories of the university. Rarely had so many national flags been burned by so many foreigners resolved on finishing once and for all with the symbols of the state, before finishing with the state itself. The French government knew how to answer this internationalism, turning over to the prisons of every country the Spaniards, Iranians, Tunisians, Portuguese, Africans and all those who had dreamed in France of a freedom forbidden in their homelands.

All the chatter about partial demands could never efface a single moment of lived freedom. In a few days the certainty of possible global change reached a point of no return. Hierarchical organization, hit at its economic foundations, ceased to appear as inevitable. The refusal of leaders and monitors, like the struggle against the state and its police, had first become a reality in the workplaces, where employers and managers at every level had been kicked out. Even the presence of managerial apprentices (the men of the trade unions and parties), could not efface from the minds of revolutionaries that what had been done with the greatest passion had been done without leaders, and therefore against them. The term "Stalinist" was thus recognized by everyone as the worst insult in the political spectrum.

The work stoppages, as the essential phase of a movement that was hardly unaware of its insurrectionary character, reminded everyone of the primordial banality that alienated work produced alienation. The right to be lazy was affirmed not only in popular graffiti like "NEVER WORK" or "LIVE WITHOUT DEAD TIME, ENJOY WITHOUT RESTRAINT," but above all in the unleashing of playful activity. Fourier had already remarked how it took workers several hours to put up a barricade that rioters could erect in a few minutes. The disappearance of forced labor necessarily coincided with the free flow of cre-

"END THE UNIVERSITY!"
Council for the Maintenance of the Occupations

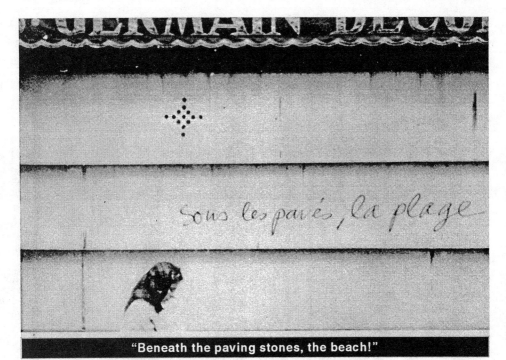

"Beneath the paving stones, the beach!"

ativity in every sphere: graffiti, language, behavior, tactics, street fighting techniques, agitation, songs and posters, comic strips. Everyone was thus able to measure the amount of creative energy that had been crushed during the periods of survival, the days condemned to production, shopping, television, and to passivity erected as a principle. It's with the same geiger-counter that we can estimate the sadness of the leisure factories where we pay to consume, in boredom, commodities we produce in the weariness that makes leisure desirable.

"BENEATH THE PAVING STONES, THE BEACH," joyously proclaimed one wall-poet, while a letter apparently signed by the CNPF cynically advised the workers to forget the factory occupations and to take advantage of their wage increases by spending their holidays at the Club Méditerranée.

The commodity system was undoubtedly the target of the aggressiveness shown by the masses. While there was little looting, many storefront windows were submitted to the critique of the paving stone. The situationists had foreseen for years that the permanent incitement to accumulate the most diverse objects, in exchange for the insidious counterpart of money, would one day provoke the anger of masses abused and treated as consumption machines. Cars, which concentrated the alienation of work and leisure, mechanical boredom, difficulty of movement and the permanent bad temper of their owners, now attracted only the match. (It is quite surprising to find

1. "You the guy talking about workers' councils in my factory?" 2. "As an elightened boss, let me remind you that the union can help with your demands." 3. "Unions are nothing but a mechanism for integrating into capitalist society!" 4. "Just like I said, miss, he's a provocateur!" 5. "But we've got all the power!" "Scum!" 6. "Commodities, for which you're the servant and the cop, profit your class..." 7. "force us to the joyless labor of salaried robots and reduce life... 8. "to a succession of monotonous and disappointing objects — cars, TV, leisure — which guarantee our passivity..." "Watch Out!" 9. "We refuse to collaborate in our own destruction!" 10. "And I thought that elections would make them wiser. I'd better get out of here..." 11. "The proletariat must do away as quickly as possible with those who oppose its total liberation!" 12. "Comrades, as soon as we take control of the economy the power of the Workers' Councils will be the only power in the land!" Councilist-inspired comic from Toulouse.

the humanists — usually so quick to denounce violence — reluctant to applaud this healthy gesture, saving from death the large numbers of people doomed each day to accidents on the roads.) The shortage of money caused by the closing of the banks was felt not as a nuisance, but as an easing of human relationships. Towards the end of May people began to get used to the idea of the disappearance of money. Effective solidarity was alleviating the shortages in individual situations. Free food was distributed in many places by the strikers. Moreover, everyone was aware that in the event of a long strike it would be necessary to begin requisitions, and so to usher in a period of real abundance.

This way of seizing things at the root was truly realized theory and the practical refusal of ideology — to such an extent that those who were acting in so radical a fashion were doubly enabled to denounce the distortion of reality of those who operated in their palace of mirrors: the bureaucratic machines that struggled to impose their own reflection everywhere. Thus, those who fought for the most advanced objectives of the revolutionary project were able to speak in the name of everyone and from real knowledge. They were most keenly aware of the distance between the practice of the rank-and-file and the ideas of the leaders. From the first assemblies in the Sorbonne, those who claimed to speak in the name of a traditional group and specialized politics found themselves roundly booed, and hurried from the floor. The people fighting on the barricades never deemed it necessary to hear an explanation, by confirmed or potential bureaucrats, as to who they were fighting for. They knew well enough, from the pleasure that they took in combat, that they were fighting for themselves, and that was all they needed. They were the motor force of the revolution which no apparatus can tolerate. It was mostly against them that the brakes were used.

The critique of everyday life successfully began to modify the landscape of alienation. The Rue Gay-Lussac was named the Rue du 11 Mai, red and black flags gave a human appearance to the fronts of public buildings. The Haussmannian perspective of the boulevards was corrected and the green belts redistributed and closed to traffic. Everyone, in his own way, made his own critique of urbanism. As for the critique of the artistic project, it was not to be found among the travelling salesmen of the happenings or the cold leftovers of the avant garde, but in the streets, on the walls, and in the general movement of emancipation which carried within itself even the realization of art. Doctors, so often attached to the defense of corporate interests, passed into the camp of the revolution with a denunciation of the police functions forced upon them: "Capitalist society, under the cover of apparent neutrality (liberalism, medical vocation, non-combatant humanism) has put the doctor on the side of repression: he is charged with keeping the population fit for work and consumption (e.g. industrial medicine) and with making people accept a society that makes them sick (e.g. psychiatry)." It was the honor of the interns and nurses of the Sainte-Anne psychiatric hospital to denounce in practice that nightmare universe by occupying the buildings, chasing off the excrement whose demise Breton dreamed of, and taking into the occupation committee representatives of the so-called "sick."

Rarely had anyone seen so many people question so many platitudes, and undoubtedly it will one day be necessary to affirm that in May 1968 a sense of profound upheaval preceded the real transformation of the world and of life. A *manifestly councilist* attitude had thus everywhere preceded the appearance of councils. But what the new recruits of the new proletariat can accomplish will be done even better by the workers once they get out of the cages where they are kept by the monkeys of trade unionism: that is to say, soon, if one keeps in mind slogans such as "LYNCH SEGUY."

The formation of action committees by the rank-and-file was a distinctive and positive sign of the movement. Nonetheless, most of the obstacles which were trying to break the movement led to their collapse. The committees originated in a profound desire to escape bureaucratic manipulations and to begin independent action at the base in the framework of general subversion. Thus the action committees formed in the Rhône–Poulenc factories, in the NMPP, and in certain stores, to cite only a few, were able from the beginning to launch and consolidate the strike against all maneuvers of the unions. This was also the case with the "worker–student" action committees,

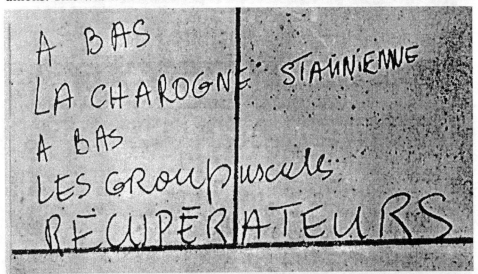

"Down with Stalinist dead meat! Down with the recuperators!"

QUE PEUT LE MOUVEMENT REVOLUTIONNAIRE MAINTENANT?

TOUT

QUE DEVIENT-IL ENTRE LES MAINS DES PARTIS ET DES SYNDICATS?

RIEN

QUE VEUT-IL? LA REALISATION DE LA SOCIETE SANS CLASSE PAR LE POUVOIR DES CONSEILS OUVRIERS

conseil pour le maintien des occupations

"What can the revolutionary movement do now? Everything. What becomes of it in the hands of the parties and unions? Nothing. What does the movement want? The realization of a classless society through the power of workers' councils."
Council for the Maintenance of Occupations

which were able to accelerate the extension and reinforcement of the strike. Nevertheless, because they were set up by "militants," the form of these committees suffered from their impoverished origins. Most of them were easy targets for the specialists of infiltration: they let themselves be paralyzed by sectarian quarrels, which could only discourage naive people with good intentions. Many committees disappeared in this way. Others nauseated the workers with their eclecticism and ideology. Without any direct relationship to real struggles, the formation was a bastardized by-product of revolutionary action, giving rise to all sorts of caricatures and recuperations (e.g. Odéon Action Committee, Writers' Action Committee, etc.).

The working class had spontaneously realized what no trade union or party could do or wanted to do for it: it had launched the strike and occupied the factories. It had done the essential, without which nothing would have been possible, but it did nothing more, and thus gave outside forces the chance to dispossess it and speak in its name. Stalinism played its most brilliant role since Budapest. The so-called Communist Party and its trade-union annex constituted the main counter-revolutionary force holding back the movement. Neither the bourgeoisie nor the social democrats could have fought so effectively. It was precisely because the CGT had the most powerful organization and could administer the largest dose of illusions that it appeared all the more obviously as the major enemy of the strike. In fact all the unions pursued the same goal. None of them, however, attained the poetry of *L'Humanité*, which ran the indignant headline: "GOVERNMENT AND EMPLOYERS PROLONG STRIKE."

In modern capitalist society the trade unions are neither degenerated working-class organizations nor revolutionary ones betrayed by bureaucratic leaders, but are mechanisms for the integration of the proletariat into the system of exploitation. Reformist in its essence, the trade union – regardless of the political content of the bureaucracy which runs it – remains the best bulwark for management. (This was perfectly demonstrated by the socialist unions in the sabotage of the great Belgian wildcat strike of 1960–61.) It is the principle obstacle between the proletariat and total emancipation. From now on any revolt by the working class will be made against its own unions. It was this elementary truth that the neo-Bolsheviks refused to recognize.

Thus, even while calling for revolution, they remained on counter-revolutionary ground. Trotskyists and Maoists of every stripe have always defined themselves in relation to official Stalinism. By that very fact they helped to nourish the illusions of the proletariat about the Communist Party and the trade unions. Thus it was no surprise to hear them crying once more about betrayal where there was nothing but the natural conduct of a bureaucracy. Behind their defense of "more revolutionary" unions was the secret dream of one day infiltrating them. Not only because they could not see what was modern but because they persist in reproducing all the revolutions of our era: from 1917 to the peasant–bureaucratic revolutions of China and Cuba. The strength of their anti-historical inertia weighed heavily in the scales of counter-revolution, and their ideological prose helped to falsify the real dialogues that were beginning everywhere.

But all these objective obstacles, external to the action and consciousness of the working class, would not have survived the first factory occupation if the proletariat's own subjective obstacles were not already there. The revolutionary current that mobilized millions of workers in a few days had come a long way. Decades of counter-revolutionary history are not borne with impunity. Something always remains, and this time it was the backwardness of theoretical consciousness that had the most serious consequences. Consumer alienation, spectacular passivity, and organized separation have been the major accomplishments of modern affluence. It was these aspects

1. 'Assholes! Schmucks! Scum! Pigs! Rejects! Sons of bitches!'
2. 'Shitheads! No balls! Fascists! Assassins! Impotents!'
3. 'Fuck-ups! Cunts! Jerks! Cops! Patriots!'
4. 'Vermin! Roaches! Paranoids! Get back to your shitcans!'
5. 'Turds! Cowards! Priests! Castrates!'
6. 'That's enough! I'm a worker, too!' 'Piss off, shithead! Ha! Ha! Ha!'

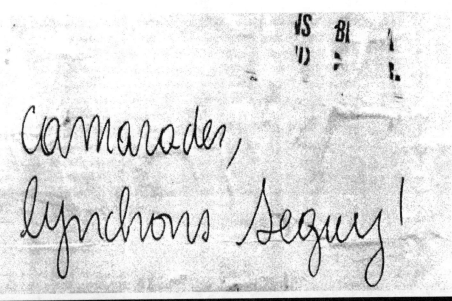

"Comrades, let's lynch Seguy!"

which were first of all challenged by the May uprising, but it was the hidden side of the very consciousness of people which saved the old world. The workers entered the struggle spontaneously, armed only with their subjectivity in revolt. The depth and violence of the revolt was their immediate reply to the unbearable dominant order. But in the last analysis the revolutionary mass did not have the time for an exact and real consciousness of what it was doing. And it is this inadequate relation between theory and practice which remains the fundamental trait of proletarian revolutions which fail. Historical consciousness is an essential condition of social revolution. Of course, conscious groups grasped the deeper meaning of the movement and understood its development, and it was they who acted with the most radicalism and effect. For it was not radical ideas that were lacking, but a coherent and organized theory.

Those who spoke of Marcuse as the "theoretician" of the movement didn't know what they were talking about. They didn't understand the movement itself, let alone Marcuse. Marcusian *ideology*, already ridiculous, was pasted onto the movement in the same way that Geismar, Sauvageot and Cohn-Bendit had been "designated" to represent it. But even they confessed an ignorance of Marcuse.[4] In reality, if the revolutionary crisis of May showed anything it was precisely the opposite of Marcuse's theses: that the proletariat had not been integrated, and is the major revolutionary force in modern society. Pessimists and sociologists have to do their homework again, along with the mouthpieces of underdevelopment, Black Power and Dutschkeism.

1. 'You hear that somebody just shot Bob Kennedy?'
2. 'That's a professional risk.' 'Well, somebody's got to govern!'
3. 'Miserable asshole! We can rule ourselves! Death to all leaders!'

It was also this theoretical backwardness that gave rise to all those practical weaknesses that paralyzed the struggle. If the principle of private property, the basis of bourgeois society, was everywhere trampled upon, those who dared to go all the way were very rare. The refusal to loot was only a detail: nowhere did the workers go on to distribute the commodities in the big stores. The reopening of certain sectors of production and distribution for the use of the strikers was never attempted, despite some isolated calls in favor of such a perspective. In fact, such an undertaking already presupposed another form of proletarian organization than that of the trade-union police. And it was this autonomous form that was so cruelly lacking.

If the proletariat cannot organize itself in a revolutionary way it cannot win. The Trotskyist moans about the absence of a "vanguard organization" are an inversion of the historical project of the emancipation of the proletariat. The accession of the working class to historical consciousness will be the task of the workers themselves, and that will be possible only through an autonomous organization. The form of the council remains the means and goal of total emancipation.

1. 'Comrades, the radio is broadcasting back-to-work calls!'
2. 'If they think they've won, they're wrong!'
3. 'They're toying with us, but not for much longer!'

It was these subjective obstacles that prevented the working class from speaking for itself and which let the phrase-specialists, who were most directly responsible for these obstacles, go on pontificating. But wherever they encountered radical theory they suffered. Never had so many people, with such justification, been treated as *rabble*: aside from the official spokesmen of Stalinism, it was the Axeloses, the Godards, the Châtelets, the Morins,[5] and the Lapassades who found themselves insulted and chased off in the amphitheaters and streets when they turned up to pursue their careers. It is certain that these reptiles took no chances of dying from embarrassment. They awaited their hour, the defeat of the occupation movement, to take up the old numbers once again. In the program of the ridiculous "Summer University" (*Le Monde*, July 3rd) we found, once again, Lapassade on self-management, Lyotard and Châtelet on contemporary philosophy and Godard, Sartre and Butor on its "support committee."

Obviously, all those who had been obstacles to the revolutionary transformation of the world had not been transformed one bit. Just as unshakable as the Stalinists, who had nothing to say about an ominous movement except that it had cost them the elections, the Leninists of the Trotskyist groups saw it only as a confirmation of their thesis on the lack of a vanguard party. As for the mob of spectators, they collected or sold off the revolutionary publications, and ran to buy posters blown up from photographs of the barricades.

Notes

[1] A factory in the western suburbs made walkie-talkie radios for the use of the demonstrators. The post office employees in several cities assured communications for the strikers.

[2] From *Medicine and Repression*, a text put out by the National Center of Young Doctors.

[3] A tract issued on June 8th, quoted in ICO No. 72, signed by the delegate of a Swedish worker–student solidarity committee in Göteborg, reported that Tomasi, the CGT representative at Renault, refused their contribution, arguing that "the current strike is a *French affair* and doesn't concern other countries, that the French workers were sufficiently advanced and therefore lacked nothing, especially money... that the present crisis was in no way revolutionary, that the only issues were the 'demands,' that the running of the factories by the workers themselves was a romantic idea unrelated to the French situation, that the strike was the result of long years of quiet and patient work by the trade unions, and, finally, that small groups of *infiltrators* were unfortunately trying to turn the workers against their own leaders by persuading them that the unions had followed the workers into the strike and not the other way around."

[4] Although they have in fact read very little, these intellectual recuperators do not shrink from hiding their reading in order to pose as pure men of action. By postulating an independence that would come from action they hope it will be forgotten that they were only publicity's puppets in a *represented* action. What other conclusions could be drawn from the cynical declaration of Geismar in *La Révolte étudiante* (Éditions du Seuil): "*Perhaps in twenty years, if we succeed in building a new society and a new university in that society,* historians and ideologues will discover the creative sources of what is going to happen in a handful of little works and pamphlets written by philosophers and other men, but I think for the time being these sources are unimportant." The clumsy Geismar can take off his moustache. He has been recognized!

[5] This swine is going too far. In his idiotic book *Mai 1968: la brèche*, he doesn't shrink from accusing the situationists of ganging up "several against one" in some fights. The lie is definitely a profession with this former contributor to *Arguments*. He nonetheless should know that a single situationist could chase him all the way to Versailles, or even Plodemet.

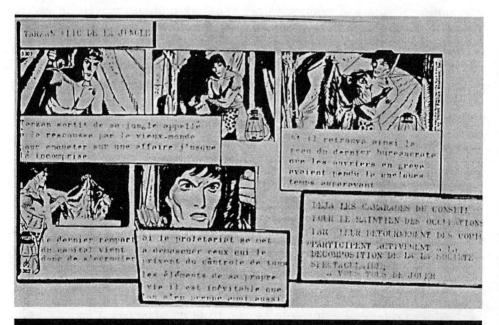

"TARZAN, JUNGLE COP"
"Tarzan came out of the jungle at the request of the old world order to investigate the unresolved situation. He finds the skin of the last bureaucrat hung by the workers. Capital's last protecting wall has just collapsed. 'If the proletariat unmasks those who deprive them from control of their own life, they'll find me, too.' Already, comrades of the Occupation Committee participate actively in the decomposition of spectacular society by détourning comics! The game is in your hands!"

7
The High Point

Let us conclude: those who are unable to change methods when the times demand it doubtless prosper as long as they remain in step with fortune; but they are lost as soon as fortune changes. As for the rest I think it is better to be too bold than too cautious...

Machiavelli, *The Prince*

On the morning of May 27th Seguy went to announce to the workers at Renault-Billancourt the agreement concluded between the unions, the government and the employers. The workers unanimously shouted down the bureaucrat, who, as his whole speech showed, had come in hopes of having himself acclaimed for these results. Confronted with the anger of the rank-and-file, the Stalinists suddenly took shelter behind a detail which had been suppressed up to that point, and which was in fact essential – nothing would be signed without the ratification of the workers. Since the workers had rejected the agreement, the strike and negotiations would go on. Following Renault, all sectors rejected the crumbs with which the bourgeoisie and its auxiliaries thought they could purchase the resumption of work.

The content of the "Grenelle Agreement" certainly had little enough to arouse the enthusiasm of the working masses who knew they were virtually masters of production, which they had paralyzed for ten days. The agreement raised wages by seven per cent and lifted the legally guaranteed minimum wage (SMIG – *salaire minimum integral garanti*) from 2.22 to 3.00 francs. This would mean that the most exploited sector of the working class, particularly in the provinces, those earning 348.80 francs a month, would now have a purchasing power more suited to the "affluent society" – 520 francs a month. The days lost in the strike would not be paid until they were made up in overtime. This tip would already be a heavy burden on the normal functioning of the French economy, especially in its obligations to the Common Market and other aspects of international capitalist competition. All the workers knew that such "benefits" would be taken back in kind with imminent price rises. They *felt* that it would be much more expedient to sweep away the system which had already conceded all it could, and to organize society on a new basis. The fll of the Gaullist regime was necessarily the prerequisite for this reversal of perspective.

The Stalinists understood how dangerous the situation was. Despite their constant support, the government had just failed once more to reestablish itself. After Pompidou's failure on May 11th to check the crisis by sacrificing his authority in the domain of the university, a speech by de Gaulle and the hastily concluded agreement between Pompidou and the unions had failed to circumvent a crisis that had become profoundly social. The Stalinists began to despair of the survival of Gaullism, since they had been unable to save it up till then, and because Gaullism seemed to have lost the elasticity essential to its survival. They found themselves obliged, much to their regret, to run the risk of being in the other camp – where they had always claimed to be. On the 28th and 29th of May they gambled all on the fall of Gaullism. They had come to terms with many pressures, mainly those of the workers, and subsequently of those oppositional elements who began clamoring for the replacement of Gaullism, and thus could have been joined by those who first and foremost wanted the regime to fall. These included the Christian trade unionists of the CFDT, Mendès-France, the dim-witted Mitterrand's

1. "The Enragés and Situationists publish very funny comics!" "Curiously, they just change the balloons!" "Isn't this a new concept for revolutionary praxis?" 2. "Sure, the détournement of comics, which is a proletarian form of graphic expression, realizes the supercession of bourgeois art." 3. A few seconds later... "Please don't shoot!" "Yup! Why not, stupid assholes! We're too lazy to draw the pictures!"

"Nanterre was quiet. Blue remained grey because nobody reinvented it.
1. 'Fuck Morin and Lefebvre!' 'And we'll get Touraine, too!' The Enragés,
campus punks, wanted to break the equanimity of the dialogue.
2. January 26, 1968. In order to protect plain-clothes cops, billy-clubbed
Grappin called out the regular cops, who were thrown back by various projectiles. 3. But pretty quickly, boredom resurfaced. 'What a nice cafeteria!'
'Oh, Alain, it's paradise!' 'Well, there's a shortage of revolutionary boys!'
'To fuck the co-eds? You must be joking!' Just when some people started
to remember the future... 4. On March 22, nothing happened. The
ultra-left militant rascals decided to share their misery. 5. All the old
liars were there: the anarchists-in-residence, and even some Stalinists.
The Enragés took off, insulting their audience. 6. 'Only shitheads
ideologize!' The evening ended agreeably in a bar near Les Halles.
7. Of course, Cohn-Bendit is no leader..."

"Federation," as well as the crowd that turned out at Charléty stadium for the formation of an ultra-leftist bureaucratic organization.[1] All these dreamers were raising their voices only in the name of the supposed forces that the Stalinists would put into play to open the way for *their* brand of post-Gaullism, mutterings which events immediately revealed as ridiculous.

The Stalinists were much more realistic. They resigned themselves to asking for a "popular government" in the powerful and numerous demonstrations staged by the CGT on the 29th, and were already preparing to defend it. They knew perfectly well that such a government would only be a dangerous last resort. While they were still able to help defeat the revolutionary movement before it succeeded in overthrowing Gaullism, they rightly feared that they would be unable to defeat it *afterwards*. On the 28th of May, an editorial broadcast on the radio had already contended, with a premature pessimism, that "the French Communist Party would never rise again," and that the principal danger now lay with the "situationist leftists."

On May 30th a speech by de Gaulle firmly underlined his intention to stay in power, whatever the price. He offered a choice between the coming elections or immediate civil war. Trusted regiments were deployed around Paris and abundantly photographed. The overjoyed Stalinists had no trouble restraining themselves from calling for an extension of the strike to bring down the old regime. They eagerly rallied to the Gaullist elections, no matter what the price would be to themselves.

In such conditions the alternatives were irrevocably posed: the autonomous affirmation of the proletariat, or the complete defeat of the movement — a revolution of the councils or the Grenelle Agreement. The revolutionary movement could not settle accounts with the French Communist Party without first throwing out de Gaulle. The form of workers' power which would have been developed in the post-Gaullist phase of the crisis, being blocked by both the old state reaffirmed and the Communist Party, no longer had any hope of reversing its approaching defeat.

Note

[1] It was to the credit of the Cohn-Bendit faction of the March 22nd Movement that they refused the advances of the renegade Stalinist Barjonet and other ecumenical leftist small-timers. It goes without saying that the situationists, for their part, responded only with contempt. (See the *Address to all Workers* by the Comité pour le Maintien des Occupations.)

8

The "Council for the Maintenance of Occupations" and Councilist Tendencies

> This explosion was provoked by groups in revolt against modern consumer and technical society, whether it be the communism of the East or the capitalism of the West. They are groups, moreover, which have no idea at all of what they would replace it with, but who delight in negation, destruction, violence, anarchy, and who brandish the black flag!
>
> De Gaulle, Televised speech of June 7th, 1968

The "Council for the Maintenance of Occupations (CMDO)" was formed on the evening of May 17th by those supporters of the first Occupation Committee of the Sorbonne who had left with it and who proposed to uphold for the rest of the crisis the program of council democracy which was inseparable from a quantitative and qualitative expansion of the occupation movement.

About forty people were continuously associated with the CMDO, and they were joined for a while by other revolutionaries and strikers coming

1. 'A good bureaucratic-revolutionary fix of the elections and we'll be out of this mess.! 2. 'What the people want is to be led! To each his job! I govern, the masses obey!' 3. 'You're too optimistic. The workers won't have it any more. Our future is threatened. If you'd read Marx, you'd understand!'

from various industries, from the provinces, or from abroad and returning there. The CMDO was more or less constantly made up of about ten situationists and Enragés (among them Debord, Khayati, Riesel and Vaneigem) and as many workers, high-school students or "students," and other councilists without specific social functions.

Throughout its existence the CMDO was a successful experiment in direct democracy, guaranteed by an equal participation of everyone in debates, and the decisions and their execution. It was essentially an uninterrupted general assembly, deliberating day and night. No faction or private meetings ever existed outside the common debate.

A unit spontaneously created in the conditions of a revolutionary moment, the CMDO was obviously less of a council than a councilist organization, thus functioning on the model of *soviet democracy*. As an improvised response to that precise moment, the CMDO could neither present itself as a permanent councilist organization, nor try to transform itself into an organization of that kind. Nonetheless, an almost general agreement on the major situationist theses reinforced its cohesion.

Three commissions were organized within the general assembly to facilitate its practical activity. The Printing Commission took charge of the production and printing of CMDO publications, both in operating the machines to which it had access and in collaboration with strikers from certain print shops. The Liaison Commission, with ten cars at its disposal, took care of contacts with occupied factories and the delivery of material for distribution. The Requisitions Commission, which excelled during the most difficult period, made sure that paper, gasoline, food, money, and wine were never lacking.

There was no permanent committee to ensure rapid writing of the texts, whose content was determined by everyone, but on each occasion several members were designated, who then submitted the result to the assembly.

The CMDO itself occupied the buildings of the National Pedagogical Institute on the Rue d'Ulm, beginning on May 19th. At the end of May it moved to the basement of the building next door, a "School of Decorative Arts." The occupation of the institute was of interest in that, while educators of all kinds were being denounced and ridiculed in their miserable profession, large groups of employees, workers, and technicians seized the occasion to demand control of the workplace and valiantly supported the movement in all its forms of struggle.[1] Thus the equal-representation committee of occupation found itself in the hands of revolutionaries. An Enragé from Nanterre was put in charge of security. The whole world congratulated itself on that choice, even the teachers. Democratic order was disturbed by no-one, which made the greatest tolerance possible: one of the Stalinist employees was even allowed to sell *L'Humanité* at the door. The red and black flags flew side-by-side on the front of the building.

The CMDO published a certain number of texts. On May 19th, *A Report on the Occupation of the Sorbonne* concluded

> The student struggle has now been superseded. Even more superseded are all candidates for bureaucratic promotion who think it clever to feign respect for the Stalinists at the very moment when the CGT and the so-called Communist Party are *trembling*. The outcome of the current crisis is in the hands of the workers themselves if they successfully accomplish the occupation of their factories, what the occupation of the university could only outline.

On May 22nd, the declaration *For the Power of the Workers Councils* stated:

> In ten days, not only have hundreds of factories been spontaneously occupied by the workers and a spontaneous general strike totally disrupted the activity of the country, but, moreover, several buildings belonging to the state have been occupied by *de facto* commit-

(Cartoon spread on the following pages): "Survival and its False Dilemmas" [text from Raoul Vaneigem's *Treatise on How to Live, for the Use of the Young*] 1. 'Survival is life reduced to economic imperatives.' 2. 'Survival today, then, is life reduced to consumption.' 3. 'Things today give the answer, Supercession, even before the so-called revolution thinks up the question.' 4. 'What is not superceded rots, and what rots in turn stimulates supercession.' 5. 'Ignoring both, refusal accelerates decomposition and becomes a part of it, again favoring supercession.' 6. 'As one sometimes says of a murder victim.... '7. 'He made the murderer's job easier.' 8. 'Survival is what results when not superceding becomes intolerable.' 9. 'A simple refusal of survival condemns us to powerlessness.' 10. 'It didn't work.' 'Sure looks like it.' 11. 'From then on... one must go back to the nexus of radical demands.' 12. 'Abandonned by the initially revolutionary movements.'

La survie et sa fausse contestation

TRAITE DE SAVOIR-VIVRE A L'USAGE DES JEUNES GENERATIONS
par Raoul Vaneigem

(Gallimard)

La survie est la vie réduite aux impérat économique

Ce qui n'est pas dépassé pourrit,

ce qui pourrit incite au dépassement.

Ignorant l'un et l'autre mouvem le refus en porte à faux accélè la décomposition et s'y intègre,

La survie est le non-dépassement devenu invivable.

Le simple refus de la survie condamne à l'impuissance.

Ça n'a pas fonctionné !

On le dirait !

tees who are taking control. In such a situation, which in any case can't last but which confronts the alternative of extending itself or disappearing, all the old ideas are swept aside and all radical hypotheses on the return of the revolutionary movement confirmed.

This text enumerated three possibilities, in order of decreasing probability: An agreement between the government and the Communist Party "on the demobilization of the workers in exchange for economic benefits"; the coming to power of the left "which will follow the same policy, albeit from a weaker position"; and, finally, the workers speaking for themselves "by becoming conscious of demands which would express the radicality of the forms of struggle they have already put into practice." They showed how the prolonging of the current situation could contain such a perspective:

> The need to reopen certain sectors of the economy under workers' control can lay the basis for this new power, which takes everything beyond the limits of the existing parties and trade unions. It will be necessary to put the railways and printing presses back into operation to serve the needs of the workers' struggle. It will be necessary for the new *de facto* authorities to requisition and distribute food.

On May 30th, the *Address to all Workers* declared:

> What we have done in France now haunts Europe. Soon it will threaten all the ruling classes of the world, from the bureaucrats of Moscow and Peking to the millionaires of Washington and Tokyo. *Just as we have made Paris dance*, the international proletariat will again take up arms against every capital city of every state, every citadel of every alienation. The occupation of factories and of the government buildings throughout the entire country hasn't just stopped the economy, it has called the whole meaning of social life into question. Almost everybody wants to stop living this way. We are already a revolutionary movement. All we need is the widespread *consciousness of what we have already done*, and we will be the masters of this revolution... Those who turned down the ridiculous contract agreements offered them (agreements that overjoyed the trade-union leaders) have still to discover that while they cannot 'receive" much more within the framework of the existing economy, they can *take everything* if they transform the very bases of the economy on their own behalf. The bosses can hardly pay more — but they could disappear.

The rest of the *Address* rejected the "bureaucratic–revolutionary replastering" which attempted at Charlety to bring together all the small leftist groups, and refused the hand which the dissident Stalinist André Barjonet shamelessly extended to the situationists. The *Address* showed that the power of the workers' councils was the only revolutionary solution, one that had already made its mark in the class struggles of this century. Later, intervening in the struggle at Flins, on June 8th the CMDO issued the tract *It's Not Over*, which denounced the methods and aims of the unions in the affair:

> The trades unions are ignorant of the class struggle; know only the laws of the market, and in their dealings claim to own the workers... The shameful maneuver to prevent reinforcements from reaching the workers at Flins is only one more repugnant 'victory' for the unions in their struggle against the general strike... No unity with those dividing us.

The CMDO also published a certain number of posters, about fifty comic strips, and several appropriate songs. Its major tracts had printings of between 150,000 and 200,000 copies. Naturally, trying to bring its practice and its theory into agreement, the CMDO contacted the workers of the occupied print shops, who gladly put the excellent machinery at their disposal back into operation (it is well known that the independent printers are less dominated by Stalinists than those of the press). The texts were also frequently reproduced in the provinces and abroad, immediately on arrival of the first copies.[2] The CMDO itself took responsibility for their translation and first printing in English, German, Spanish, Italian, Danish, and Arabic. The versions in Arabic and Spanish were first distributed among immigrant laborers. A falsified version of the *Address* was reprinted in *Combat* on June

(Cartoon spread, following): "The Proletariat as Subject and as Representation" [text from Guy Debord's book, Society of the Spectacle]

1. 'Proletarian revolution depends completely on this necessity...
2. that for the first time theory... 3. as the intelligence of human praxis, must be acknowledged and expanded by the masses.' 4. 'This theory demands that workers become dialecticians... 5. inscribing their thought into praxis...
6. therefore it demands more from men without quality... 7. than the bourgeois revolution demanded from those qualified men that it employed:...
8. because the partial ideological consciousness erected by a segment of the bourgeoisie... 9. rested on the central core of social life, the economy...
10. in which this class had already gained power.' 11. 'So the very development of class society into organized spectacularity forces the revolutionary project to become visibly what it already was essentially.'

ur la première fois, c'est la théorie

en tant qu'intelligence de la pratique humaine qui doit être reconnue et vécue par les masses.

ainsi elle demande aux *hommes sans qualité*

bien plus que la révolution bourgeoise ne demandait aux hommes qualifiés qu'elle déléguait à sa mise en œuvre :

dans laquelle cette classe *était déjà au pouvoir.*

Le développement même de la société de classes jusqu'à l'organisation spectaculaire de la non-vie mène donc le projet révolutionnaire à devenir *visiblement* ce qu'il était déjà *essentiellement.*

3rd. The situationist references and the attacks against the Stalinists had been deleted.

Quite successfully, the CMDO tried to establish and preserve links with factories, isolated workers, action committees, and groups in the provinces. The link with Nantes was particularly well-established. Beyond that the CMDO was present in all aspects of the struggle in Paris and the suburbs.

The Council for the Maintenance of Occupations agreed to dissolve itself on the 15th of June. The ebbing of the occupation movement had led several of its members to raise the question of its dissolution a week earlier. That was delayed by the persistence of the struggles of the strikers, notably at Flins, who were refusing to accept defeat. The CMDO had never tried to get

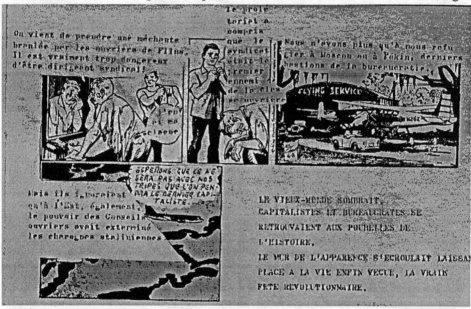

1. 'We were just beaten up by the workers in Flins. It's really too dangerous to be a union leader!' 'I'm sick of it!' 2. 'The proletariat understands that unions are their first enemy.' 3. 'Well, we'll just seek asylum in Moscow or Peking, the last bastions of bureaucracy.' 4. But they didn't know that in the Eastern bloc the power of the workers' councils had already wiped out the Stalinist dead meat. 'Let's hope that it's not with our guts that they hang the last capitalist.' The old world was sinking. Capitalists and bureaucrats found themselves in the garbage can of history. The wall of appearances crumbled, giving way to life finally lived at the true revolutionary feast.

anything for itself, not even any recruitment which aimed at a permanent existence. Its participants did not separate their personal goals from the general goals of the movement. They were independent individuals who had come together for a struggle on a determined basis at a precise moment; and who once again became independent after the struggle had ended. Some of those among them, who recognized in the Situationist International the extension of their own activity, continued to work together in that organization.[3]

Other "councilist" tendencies (in the sense that they were for the councils without wanting to recognize their theory and their truth) appeared in the buildings of the Censier annex of the Faculté des Lettres, where they held, as the "Worker–Student Action Committee," a somewhat impotent discussion which could hardly progress towards a practical clarification. Groups like "Workers' Power" and the "Workers' Liaison and Action Group," made up of many individuals from various enterprises, made the mistake of accepting into their already confused and redundant debates all kinds of adversaries or saboteurs of their positions – Trotskyists and Maoists who paralyzed the discussion, and who even publicly burned an anti-bureaucratic program drawn up by a commission assigned to the task. The councilists were able to intervene in some practical struggles, notably at the beginning of the general strike, by sending members to help in a work stoppage or to reinforce picket lines. But their interventions often suffered from defects inherent in their very grouping: often several members from a single delegation offered fundamentally conflicting perspectives to the workers. The anti-trade union group "Workers Information and Correspondence" (ICO) – which was not councilist, and was not even sure of its being a group – nonetheless met in another room. Indifferent to the situation, they rehashed the usual rubbish in their bulletin and replayed their obstructionist psychodrama: was it necessary to stick to pure news pasteurized of all theoretical germs, or was the choice of news already inseparable from the hidden theoretical presuppositions? More generally, the defect of all these groups was to draw their proud experience from past working-class defeats, and never from the new conditions and new style of the struggle which they ignored on principle. They repeated their usual *ideology* in the same boring tone that they had used during one or two decades of inactivity. They seemed to perceive nothing new in the occupation movement. They had seen it all before. They were blasé. Their knowing discouragement looked forward to nothing but defeat, so that they could publish the consequences as they had done so often before. The difference was that they had not had the chance of participating in the previous movements they had analyzed, and this time they were living the moment which they *chose* to consider in advance from the angle of the historical spectacle, or even from that of an uninstructive replay.

New councilist tendencies did not appear in the crisis, aside from the CMDO, whereas the old attitudes were completely insignificant both in theory and in practice. The March 22nd Movement, of course, had some councilist whims, as it had something of everything, but it never put them forward in its publications and its many interviews. Nonetheless, a growing audience for the call for workers' councils was manifest throughout the revolutionary crisis. That was one of the major effects, and remains one of its surest promises.

Notes

[1] One poster advised: "DON'T SAY 'TEACHER, SIR,' SAY 'DROP DEAD, ASSHOLE'!" Another reminded that "THE EDUCATOR HIMSELF MUST BE EDUCATED."

[2] Among the first reprints we can cite a Swedish pamphlet in the Libertad revolutionary series, a special issue of the clandestine Venezuelan publication, *Proletario*, and a pamphlet put out by the Japanese Zengakuren under the title *Lessons on the Defeat of the May Revolt in France.*

[3] Certain outside elements were able to claim falsely to be from the CMDO in the same way that individuals — much more frequently — claimed to be members of the S.I., whether out of sheer conceit or murkier motives. Two or three nostalgic former members of the CMDO naturally did not miss the chance to exploit their past in a miserably spectacular style. This was completely foreign to almost all the members, who contributed so many remarkable capacities without ever seeking to push themselves to the fore. The Council for the Maintenance of Occupations will return one day, with its time, which will also return.

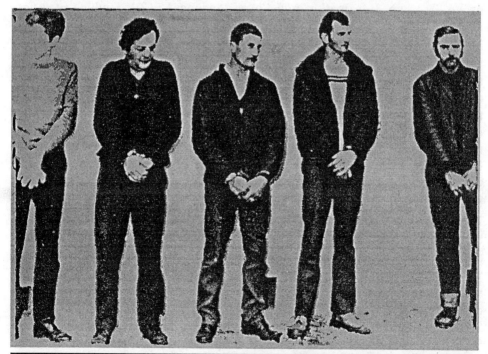

"Katangans" from the Sorbonne, arrested after being disavowed by students.

9

The State Reestablished

Everyone must raise his head, assume his responsibilities and refuse intellectual terrorism... there is no reason for the state to turn over to just anybody its administration, its public institutions, nor for it to abandon its responsibilities and forget its duties.

Robert Poujade, Speech to the
National Assembly, 24 July 1968

The bourgeoisie had waited until May 30th to openly show its support for the state. With the speech of de Gaulle the entire ruling class took back the floor and massively affirmed its presence, after having prudently hibernated behind the protection of the CRS for several weeks. The demonstration at the Concorde and on the Champs Elysées was the sub-Versaillaise response to the parades of the CGT calling for a "popular government." Reactionary hysteria flowed freely, ranging from the fear of the "Reds" to revealing slogans such as "Cohn-Bendit to Dachau!" Old veterans, survivors of all the colonial wars, ministers, ex-commandos, shopkeepers, the kittens from the 16th Arrondisement and their sugar-daddies from the better parts of town, old hacks and all those whose interests and tastes lay in senility, came out together for the defense and praise of the republic. The state thus recovered its base and the police their auxiliaries, in the UDR and the civic action committees. As soon as de Gaulle decided to remain in power a violence without cant took over from the Stalinist repression, whose task it had been up to then to clog up the revolutionary breach, mainly in the factories. After three weeks of almost total absence, the state was able to relieve its hatchet-men in the Communist Party. It put as much effort into driving the workers out of

1. "Mr. President, the factory has been freed!" 2. "We have arrested some provocateurs who cried, 'Long live the workers' councils!'
3. "Bravo, Sergeant! As long as I live, I will be the workers' council!"

the factories as the unions had put into keeping them locked up inside. De Gaulle had saved the Stalinists from the prospect of a "popular government" in which their overt role as the last enemies of the proletariat would have been so perilous. They would help him do the rest.

For both of them the question immediately became one of ending the strike and making way for the elections. The rejection of the Grenelle Agreement had taught the rulers to be wary of all negotiation at a national level. It was necessary to dismantle the strike in the same way that it had begun, sector by sector, factory by factory. The task was long and difficult. Everywhere the workers were openly hostile to the return to work. On June 5th a statement from the CGT headquarters announced that "Everywhere that essential demands have been met the interest of the workers is to come out *en masse* for a united resumption of work."

On June 6th, bank and insurance employees went back. The SNCF, a CGT bastion, also decided to go back. The trains, which had never been put at the disposal of the strikers — as the Belgian railway workers had done during the strike of 1961 — were put back into operation for the state. The first rigged ballots for the resumption of work took place at the P&T and the RATP, where only a minority of union members were allowed to vote; CGT delegates brought about the resumption of work by announcing at each station that all the others had gone back. The employees at Nation, seeing through this gross maneuver, immediately stopped work but did not succeed in relaunching the movement.

The CRS intervened similarly to expel the striking technicians at France-Inter, and to replace them with army technicians. On the 6th of June they drove the workers out of the Renault factory at Flins. This was the first attempt, other than by ideology, to break the strike, which was still complete in the steel industry: the strike-breakers moved in, gun in hand. "The time for marches is over," wrote the Flins strikers in their call for the re-occupation of their factory, on June 6th. They realized at that moment just how destructive was the isolation they had put up with. Thousands of revolutionaries responded to their call, but only a few hundred were able to join them and fight at their sides. At the meeting organized by the unions at Elizabethville the workers forced the CGT delegate to allow Geismar, a member of the March 22nd Movement, to speak, not out of any feeling for his particular importance, but out of a simple concern for democracy.

The police attacked at 10 A.M. For twelve hours, two thousand workers and students fought it out with four thousand police and CRS in the streets and fields of the neighboring towns. They waited in vain for reinforcements from Paris. In fact the CGT had prevented the departure of the workers from Boulogne–Billancourt[1] and kept the trains at the Gare Saint-Lazare from being put at the disposal of the thousands of demonstrators who had rushed there for the fight at Flins. The organizers of the demonstration, with Geismar and Sauvageot in the lead, were just as brilliant. They backed down to the CGT and finished the work it had begun by dissuading those who thought they were going to the aid of Flins from taking over a train, and calling on them to disperse after the first scuffles with the police. For all that, the miserable Geismar got no thanks for his efforts. This bore was still treated as a "specialist in provocation" in a particularly foul communication from the CGT, which did not hesitate to call the Flins revolutionaries "groups foreign to the working class"; "paramilitary formations who have already made an appearance in similar operations in the Paris region" and who were "obviously acting in the interests of the worst enemies of the working class," for "it is hard to believe that the arrogance of the management in the steel industry, the support it is receiving from the government, the police brutality

1. "The comrades entrusted me with this letter for you."
2. "We did well, Monsignor, to launch the idea of self-management...
Let's see what those brave workers think about it."
3. " 'Scumbags! Don't mess around with this business or we'll fuck you up!' "

against the workers, and the attempts at provocation are not a concerted effort."

The unions were able to bring about the resumption of work almost everywhere; they had already been thrown some crumbs. Only the workers in the steel industry continued to hold out. After the setback at Flins the state was still going to take its chances at the Peugeot plant at Sochaux. On June 11th, the CRS attacked the workers. The confrontation was quite violent and lasted several hours. For the first time in this extended crisis the forces of order fired into the crowd. Two workers were killed. The time had come when the authorities could act without provoking any reaction. The movement was already defeated and the political repression was beginning. Nonetheless, on June 12th, in the wake of the death of a high-school student at Flins, one last night of rioting saw several innovations: the rapid multiplication of barricades and the systematic bombardment of the police with Molotov cocktails thrown from the roofs.

On the following day the State decreed the disbandment of the Maoist and Trotskyist organizations, along with the March 22nd Movement, using a law from the Popular Front period originally used against extreme right-wing paramilitary leagues.[2] Gaullism was making real overtures to the same extreme right under the table. This was the chance to recover the first May 13th — when the Fifth Republic was founded. The exiled leaders of the OAS returned to France. Salan left Tulle as the ultra-leftists were beginning to populate the redoubt of Gravelle.

There was something rotten in the air after the tricolor flags had appeared on Concorde. Merchants, provocateurs, curates, and patriots lifted their heads and returned to the streets in which they would not have dared to appear a few days before. Provocateurs in the pay of the police tried to whip up the Arabs and Jews in Belleville, and thereby provided an appropriate diversion while the mop-up operations in the factories and occupied buildings were being carried out. A campaign of calumny was stirred up around the Katangans at the Sorbonne. The pitiful leftists didn't fail to be taken in by it.

(Cartoon, left) "The Glorious Return to Work"
"After negotiating with management and the government, the union rep announces the return to work. 1. 'Stop the strike! Go back to work! We've won!' 2. But things aren't turning out that way. 'The unions have sold out! The strike must go on!' 'Long live the workers' councils!' 3. 'Stop these provocateurs! They're the true enemy of the workers!' 4. 'Long live self-management!' 'Filthy pigs! You want to protect the bureaucrats' future!' 5. 'You'll always need the unions!' 'Down with specialists! Let's throw out the reps!' 6. 'Management wouldn't put up with you if we weren't here!' 'This time we get the message. Comrades, we've got to take over ourselves!' The following week, the unions are in deep shit. Workers, organize!"

After the failure of the experiment in direct democracy, the Sorbonne had seen the rise of several fiefdoms, as preposterous as they were bureaucratic. Those the press called the "Katangans," a group of ex-mercenaries, unemployed, and *déclassés*, had quickly cut out for themselves a leadership role in

(Cartoon, left)
1. 'I've been with the JCR for a month now.' 2. 'I agreed to join one morning and had my card that same night. My life ia about to really take off.'
'How can someone be passionate about their own alienation?' 3. 'Maybe it's an attribute enforced by the military, or by sociology studies.' 4. 'Suddenly my eyes opened and I saw the horror of capitalist society... 5. I understood how alienated the working class is, and how immense is our task!' 'She's so dumb!'
6. 'In Vietnam, in Cuba, and now in Europe the world revolution predicted by Trotsky is about to happen, and I am part of it. It's fabulous!' 7. 'And tomorrow you'll marvel at the ever-renewing spectacle of local and partial revolutionary struggles to which the constant misery of your life and your insufficient criticism... 8. of the society of the spectacle will push you to participate. Capitalist society organizes the illusion of participation.
9. Bureaucratic societies have shown it how to organize this illusory participation. And you can only marvel...' 10. 'How could a worker understand one word of this vocabulary you're using?' 'You're right, demagogic workerist language was invented for the worker.' A little while later... 11. 'Tomorrow, at the museum of culture, a show on American pop art will open. You going?'
'No. Art has become the choice commodity that makes all the other commodities palatable. Besides, the boredom... 12. excreted by museums increasingly resembles the stench of the church.' 13. 'Tomorrow I'll make love with whomever I want. Tomorrow I'll play once again with the pleasures of life. Tomorrow I'll knock your teeth out, you little cunt...'

a republic of corporals. The Sorbonne thus got the masters it deserved, but even though the Katangans had already played the game of authority, they did not deserve such miserable companions. Having come there to participate in the festival they found only the pedantic providers of boredom and impotence, the Kravetzes and Peninous. The students kicked out the Katangans in the ridiculous hope that they might get permission, by such a low move, for lasting control of a disinfected Sorbonne for use as a "Summer University." One of the Katangans could rightly remark that "the students may be educated but they are not intelligent. We had come to help them out..." The retreat of the undesirables to the Odéon immediately provoked an intervention by the forces of order. The last occupants of the Sorbonne had only 48 hours to clean the walls and chase out the rats before the police arrived to let them know that the comedy was over once and for all. They left without the slightest resistance. After the defeat of the movement only imbeciles could believe that the State would not take back the Sorbonne.

In order to ensure the success of the electoral campaign it was necessary to get rid of the last islands of resistance in the steel industry. The unions, and not capital, gave in on the agreements, which allowed *L'Humanité* to applaud the "victorious resumption of work" and the CGT to call upon the steelworkers to "prolong their success by the victory of the real union of the

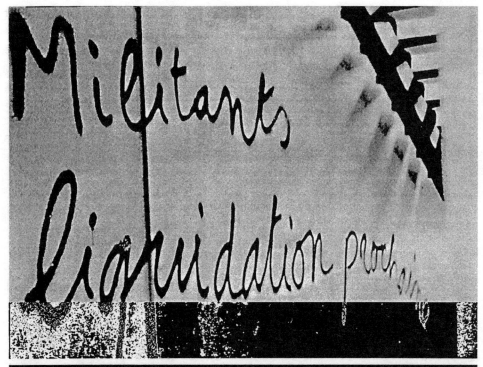

"Militants, liquidation approaches!"

forces of the left fighting around a common program in the coming elections." Renault, Rhodiaceta, and Citroën went back on the 17th and 18th. The strike was over. The workers knew that they had won almost nothing. By prolonging the strike beyond May 30th, and by taking so long to end it, they had affirmed in their own way that they wanted something other than "economic benefits." What they had wanted was revolution. But they had been unable to say it, and had no time to make it.

After the defeat it was natural that the electoral competition of the different parties of order ended in the massive victory of the party in the best position to defend it.

The Gaullist victory was accompanied by the last mop-up operations for the return to normal. All occupied buildings were evacuated. It should be noted that the State waited until the first week in July to use the fundamental juridical argument that "the occupation of buildings designated for public service of any kind is illegal." For nearly two months it had been unable to use that argument against the occupation movement. (More or less fallacious pretexts were needed by the police to justify the recapture of the Odéon, the Sorbonne and the École des Beaux Arts.)

The acts of vandalism that had marked the beginning of the movement had reemerged all the more violently at its end, showing a refusal of defeat and a firm intention to continue the struggle. Thus, to cite only two exemplary acts, readers of *Le Monde* of July 6th were informed of "carpets destroyed with eggs, butter, talcum, detergent, black paint and oil; telephones ripped out and painted red, IBM machines destroyed with hammers, windows blackened with paint, medicines strewn about and daubed with paint, records blotted out with spray paints, insulting and obscene slogans: this was the spectacle presented Wednesday morning at the medical offices (including the secretary's office and that of the Social Service, baptized by the angry inscription "Anti-Social Service"), one of the most important sections of the Sainte-Anne Neuro-Psychiatric Hospital. A scene disturbingly

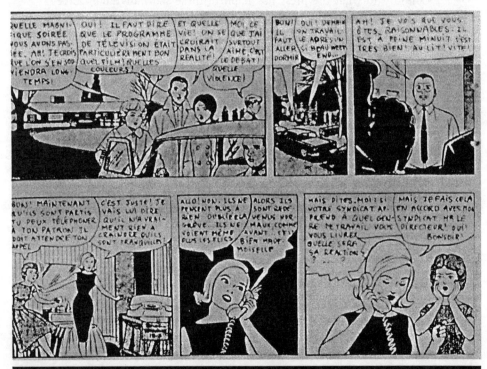

1. 'What a nice evening! Quite memorable.' 'Oh yes! I thought the TV show was particularly good. What film! What color!' 'And what a life! It could have been real!' 'I really liked the discussion. What violence!' 2. 'Okay, time for bed.' 'Yup, tomorrow, back to work after such a nice week-end.' 3. 'Ah, good kids! Only a little after midnight. To bed now, quickly!' 4. 'Okay, now that they're gone, call your boss. He must be waiting.' 'Right. I'm gonna tell him there's nothing to worry about. They're really sheep.' 5. 'Hello? No they're not planning anything any more. They've forgotten the strike, they don't even notice the cops any more.' 'Back to normal, just like before. Great.... ' 6. 'but tell me, what if you're union finds out what you're doing? How will they react?' 'But I'm doing it with their approval. Sure! Goodnight!'

similar to one in Nanterre, where the same means of devastation had been used and where slogans of the same style and spirit reappeared on all the walls... One wonders if there is not some relation between recent changes introduced in this field for strictly professional reasons and these acts of vandalism?" In *Combat* on July 2:

> Monsieur Jacquenod, headmaster of the experimental high school in Montgeron, writes: "In the general interest it is my duty to inform you of the absolutely scandalous doings recently carried out in the Essonne region by the irresponsible Enragé commandos under the influence of a certain "Situationist International." Contrary to what the press has implied, these sad individuals have proved themselves more harmful than 'colorful.' The time for benevolence is past, and the shameful degradations of monuments to the dead, churches, monasteries and public buildings which have been carried out are quite simply intolerable. After getting themselves admitted to our building on false pretexts on the night of June 13-14, they went about sticking up some 300 posters, songs, tracts, comic strips and so on. But the real damage was caused by systematic paint scribbling on the walls of the high school and technical college. On June 21, after the police had opened an inquiry, and out of sheer defiance, new degradations (posters, tracts, writings in ink) were committed in broad daylight inside the buildings." Monsieur Jacquenod judges it his duty to alert public opinion to these "acts of vandalism, quite harmful to the peaceful climate we are gradually reestablishing."

Notes

[1] On the night of June 9-10 a delegation of workers from Flins came to ask for help in the occupied factories and at Boulogne–Billancourt. The students left, but at Billancourt the CGT pickets forbade the delegates access to the factory. The tight partitions which kept the workers in the factories also separated the workers of two factories in the same industry.

[2] The pretext was badly framed, for these groups had never armed any militias. All revolutionaries will obviously show their solidarity against this sort of repression. Such measures by the police are, moreover, singularly unadapted to the character of autonomous non-hierarchical organization which proved to be the most original aspect of the movement. Numerous commentaries on the disbandment tried to assimilate the situationists to the March 22nd Movement. It was only in such circumstances, of course, that the S.I. did not publicly denounce such an assertion.

10

Perspectives for World Revolution after the Occupation Movement

The Situationist International has sown the wind.
It will reap the whirlwind.
Internationalle Situationniste, No. 8, January, 1963

The occupation movement was immediately seen throughout the world as an historical event of tremendous importance, and as the beginning of a new, menacing era whose program proclaimed the speedy death of all existing governments. A renewal of internationalism and radicalization of revolutionary tendencies was the response to the troubled stupor it created among the leaders and spokesmen of all ruling classes. The solidarity of the workers expressed itself in a number of ways — the longshoremen of Savone and Antwerp who refused to load goods going to France, the Belgian typesetters who prevented [passage of] the stillborn referendum announced by de Gaulle on May 24th by refusing to print the ballots.

Towards the middle of May the Radical Student Alliance in London sent an address to French workers and students, written in French:

We too have felt the blows of the police clubs and the effects of tear-gas; the betrayals of our so-called leaders are not unknown to us. The sum of these experiences has proved to us the necessity of joining in solidarity with the living struggles against oppressive structures in world society as well as in the universities... But you, comrades, have succeeded in pushing that struggle beyond a questioning of the class nature of the university to a struggle united with the workers which has as its goal the complete capitulation of capitalist society... Together with your comrades in the factories, in the ports, and the offices, you have destroyed the myth of the stability of capitalist Europe, and consequently you have made both the regimes and the bourgeoisie tremble with fear. In the stock markets of Europe the capitalists are trembling, professors and aging gerontocrats are turning phrases to explain the action of the masses... Comrades, you have reanimated the traditions of 1871 and 1917, you have given international socialism a new force.

The co-ordinating committee of the student strike at Columbia University published a tract in New York at the beginning of June which declared

For more than two weeks twelve million French workers and students have led a mass general strike against the same conditions which confront us in America... Despite the efforts of the trades union bureaucracies, including the "communist" leadership of the CGT, to moderate the movement and to arrive at a compromise with the employers and the Gaullist government, the workers have voted to pursue the strike until their demands are satisfied... If we win in France it will give new life to the international movement which is already manifesting itself in Germany, Spain, Italy, Japan, and even here in the United States. When we launch our own battles here we are helping to create the conditions for a victory in France and everywhere in the world. Their fight is our fight. The workers and students in France are looking to us in America for a response to their first giant step in the battle for a new society.

The barricades and Molotov cocktails of the Berkeley students, the very same who had launched the agitation in the university four years earlier, responded at the end of June. In the middle of May a revolutionary organization had been formed by the Austrian youth around the simple program of "doing the same as in France." At the end of the month occupations of university buildings had taken place in Germany, Stockholm, Brussels, and at the Hornsey Art College in London. Barricades had gone up in Rome on May 31st. In June the students of Tokyo, always combative and resolved on turning the university district into a "Latin Quarter," occupied their faculties and defended them against the police. Not even Switzerland was spared: on the

29th and 30th of June, riots broke out in Zurich, where hundreds of demonstrators armed with stones and Molotov cocktails took the major police station by assault. "The violent demonstrations in Zurich," noted *Le Monde* on July 2nd, "provoked a certain stupor. Numerous Swiss, who believed their country to be immune from the movement of opposition breaking out in Europe, were disturbed in their tranquility."

The struggle in the modern capitalist countries naturally awakened student agitation against the dictatorships and in "underdeveloped" countries. At the end of May there were violent confrontations in Buenos Aires, Dakar, Madrid, and a student strike in Peru. In June the incidents were extended to Brazil and then to Uruguay (where they culminated in a general strike), to Argentina, and to Turkey (where the universities of Istanbul and Ankara were closed until further notice), and finally to the Congo (where the high-school students demanded the suppression of exams).

The most important of the immediate results of the French movement was the first tremor against the power of the bureaucratic classes of the East,

"Live without dead time!" — "Enjoy without restraint!"

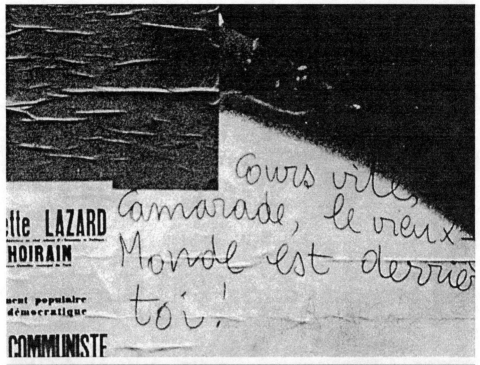

"Move quickly, comrade, the old world is right behind you!"

when Yugoslav students occupied the University of Belgrade at the beginning of June. The students formed Action committees, denounced the bureaucratic ownership of society, demanded *authentic self-management* in terms of freedom and the abolition of classes, and voted to rename the place Karl Marx University. They addressed themselves to the workers: "We are outraged by the enormous social and economic differences in our society... We are for self-management but against the enrichment of the few at the expense of the working class." Their movement met with great approval among the workers. As at the Sorbonne, "several workers also took the floor at the interminable meeting at the philosophy faculty, where speakers endlessly took turns in the general enthusiasm." (*Le Monde*, June 7th). The regime saw itself stalked to death. The demagogical self-criticism and tearful confessions of Tito, who spoke of resigning if he could not meet the just demands that had been made, showed up the weakness and the panic of the Yugoslav bureaucracy. It knows perfectly well that the radical demands of the movement, whatever maneuvers they left open for Tito himself, signalled nothing less than its own liquidation as a ruling class, and the proletarian revolution which is coming back to life, there as elsewhere. The concessions of the bureaucrats were accompanied in classical fashion with whatever dose of repression they could afford, and the usual calumnies which put forth the inverted reality of their ideology: the so-called Communist League thus denounced the "ultra-leftist radicals... eager to destroy both the democratic regime and self-management." Even *Le Monde* (June 12th) recognized that this was "the most important domestic alert that the regime had had since the war." [Since then the uprising of the Mexican students has surpassed in scale all the other responses to the French occupation movement. Mexico is a country only half-emerged from Latin American underdevelopment.]

France, too, remains in the volcanic chain of the new geography of revolution. Nothing has been settled there. The revolutionary eruption didn't come from an economic crisis, but, on the contrary, helped to create a crisis in the economy. What was attacked head-on in May was a *well-functioning capitalist economy*, but that economy, once shaken by the negative forces of its historical supercession, has to function *less well*: it thus becomes more unbearable, and reinforces its "underside," the revolutionary movement which is transforming it. The student milieu has become a permanent stronghold of disorder in French life, and this time it is no longer the disorder of a *separated* youth. The big bureaucratic machines of working-class integration paid a high price for their victory over the strike: many workers have understood. As for the small leftist groups, which were apparently reinforced (all the more so by their unnecessary disbandment by the police), they are virtually finished. The unobtrusive basket of crabs they constituted was strewn about in the limelight during the strike, but always in retreat.

The perspective of world revolution, when it reappeared in France, not only made up for the long delay of its fifty-year absence, but displayed for this reason many *premature* aspects. *Before* the occupation movement crushed the state power confronting it, it accomplished what all the revolutionary movements (except that of 1905) had achieved only *afterwards*. The armed detachments at the disposal of the government had not been defeated. And nevertheless the seizure of certain buildings and their notorious distribution among different subversive groups could not help but evoke some of the events of Barcelona in the summer of 1936. The state was *ignored* for the first time in France; this was the first practical critique of Jacobinism, for so long the nightmare of French revolutionary movements, including the Commune. In other words, radically new elements were mixed with the sudden return of the specific characteristics of French revolutions — the barricades in Paris awakening Europe. Just as it was *not enough* to simply ignore the State, there were certainly no sufficiently clear perspectives. Too few people had a coherent revolutionary theory, and its dissemination among the masses had to overcome extremely unfavorable conditions. Apart from the power of the existing order's spectacular media, there were the counter-revolutionary bureaucracies, which had at that time been unmasked by far too few. Thus no one should be surprised by the many weaknesses of the movement, but rather be amazed at its strength.

Radical theory has been confirmed and tremendously strengthened. It should now make itself known everywhere for what it is, and break all new efforts by the hard-pressed recuperators. The carriers of radical theory had had no concessions to make. They must become even more demanding from the position of strength that history has given them. Nothing short of the international power of the workers' councils can satisfy them — they can recognize no revolutionary force other than the councilist organizations which will be formed in every country. The objective conditions for revolution have become visible as soon as the revolution has begun, once again, to speak as an objective power. Now a fire has been lit which will never go out. The occupation movement has ended the sleep of the masters of commodities, and never again shall spectacular society sleep in peace.

Appendices

Documents

Section A: The Beginnings

Extracts from the platform of revolutionary "students" at Nantes, published at the start of 1968, ironically entitled:

CONTRIBUTION TO THE ELABORATION OF A MINORITY TENDENCY WITHIN THE UNEF

The defense of student interests in the face of the interests of power can only be a matter of a majority-rule unionism: a mass union in the student milieu can only be a majority one. Any assertion to the contrary is a mystification or an idiocy.

Those who want to make the student milieu a natural and objective ally of the working class, are stupid workerists, who have rather too quickly forgotten the part played by the student militias against the Spanish Republicans, the Spartakists, the Russian Soviets etc.... The only time that students as a whole can be revolutionary is during the bourgeois revolutions, e.g. 1789, 1830, 1848, Francoist Spain, fascist Greece... Sometimes students fight against Power, but this struggle has the character of a struggle in favor of bourgeois or "socializing" democracy, in other words a modern bourgeois democracy. Their struggle is that of all *avant-garde* bourgeois. It goes without saying that the young bourgeois — future lawyers, judges, doctors, licensed dealers in culture and science, the bastards of finance and industry, the priests and philosophers of Ideology, cop-psychologists, sociologists of Power, prefects and police superintendents, architects of the Sarcelles¹ of the future (this list is far from being exhaustive) — cannot ally themselves as a whole to the proletariat with a view to the latter's liberation. For such a liberation can only be for them the loss of a privileged class status. The average student who's gotten over his acne and spent his righteous juvenile revolt as a union virgin, will simply want to hurry up and finish his studies in order to pass lock, stock, and barrel into the camp of power, be immersed in material comforts and be sheltered behind diplomas and the culture of Power: the aim of the traditional student movement is, by definition, to ameliorate the student's lot, and in so doing, to allow him to move more quickly and efficiently towards the situation or career to which he's always more or less aspired, even during his "wild years."

It's important in this case to distinguish the student from the "sub-student," a relatively new product of the university, a late creation of the Fouchet Plan designed to serve the new labor demands of modern capitalism.

The fundamental aspect of the Fouchet Plan is in fact the existence of the exploited of the future, side by side with students proper...

[It] is necessary definitively to dissociate the students who will as a matter of course be exploited from those who will be lower or middle-ranking bourgeois, minor cadres, better paid than workers, but *embittered at not having been able to climb higher up the hierarchical ladder...*

Nobody can deny that the future of students proper is quite clearly a happy entree into the camp of Power...

All the managers of the Old World, whatever level they've attained in the dominant hierarchy, are ex-students.

On the other hand, the sub-students, having only the appearance of student status, will soon be proletarians, and could perhaps even be the *avant garde* of the exploited — thanks partly to what they may have gleaned from the debris of culture. Of course they will be nothing if UNEF mixes them up with the bourgeois and future bourgeois, and makes both groups believe their interests are identical and that they must both defend this artificial concept of the student condition...

The defense of the poor children of the university should not be done through complaints that seek to make them, to a greater or lesser degree, authentic participants within the bourgeois class. On the contrary, a defense should be based on joining in the struggle against Power, a struggle which gives them solidarity within their own ranks and a solidarity with the struggle led by the proletariat. They must understand that their lot is really bound up with that of the working class.

From such a perspective, maximum advantage must be taken of the system. It's a case of claiming the existing grants while demanding an increase in the amount and in their number. It's a waste of time to think up a vague theory basing allocation on a university criteria and not on a social criteria. What matters is how much cash you've got...

We should be more ambitious, not settling for counter-measures, nor for bribes in defending the student role. It should be made clear that the university, through its role in both the social and technical division of labor, has as its mission to disseminate the philosophy of Power. The content of class education is no more than the culture of that class or, when it's "neutral,," the culture that profits that class. The university for the real student is the place where he's initiated into the holy sciences and formulas which allow him and his like to be dominant in society as a cadre of the bourgeois class.

The philosophy of Power, as taught in the university or the college, obviously plays a role in society that we oppose. It's this philosophy that we find again and again directing daily life through its law and morality, which organizes and perpetuates the economic domination of the bourgeoisie (political economy) etc.

Rather than worrying about "the defense of the psychological profession," psychology students would be better off denouncing what they're being taught. Workers at odds with the social-psychologists in the factories would certainly be grateful to them in having precise information in the struggle against the new, more cunning, more subtle, forms of domination...

A GUST OF WIND THROUGH THE JAPANESE APPLE TREE[2]

Ladies and Gentlemen,

Henri Lefebvre,[3] one of the most well-known agents of recuperation of this half of the century (it's well-known how the situationists well and truly put him and the whole Arguments[4] gang in their place in their pamphlet *Into the Dustbin of History!*) proposes to add the Zengakuren[5] to his trophies. The CNRS[6] has its emissaries, PRAXIS has its researchers.

The metaphilosopher Lefebvre is less stupid than the pataphilosopher Morin. But the metastalinist ought to have the good grace to shut up when it's a matter of class struggle.

A word to the wise is enough.

Nanterre, March 19, 1968. The Enragés

GUT RAGE!

Comrades,

In spite of the proven collusion between UEC Stalinists and reactionaries, last Friday's marvellous riots show that students, in struggle, are starting to gain a consciousness that they didn't have before: and where violence begins, reformism ends. The University Council which met this morning will have its work cut out: this obsolete form of repression can do nothing to counter the violence in the streets. The banning for five years of our comrade Gerard Bigorgne from all the universities of France — quietly ignored by the whole of the press, the political groups, and students' associations — and which now menaces our comrade Rene Riesel and six other Nanterre students, is at the same time a way for the university authorities to hand them over to the police.

Faced with repression, the struggle which has begun must retain its method of violent action, which for the time being is its only strength. But above all it must instigate a consciousness amongst students who will lead the movement forward.

Because there aren't only the cops: there are also the lies of the various political tendencies — Trotskyists (JCR, FER, VO), Maoists (UJCML, CP rank and file), and anarchists-a-la-Cohn-Bendit. Let's settle our business ourselves!

The example shown by the comrades arrested at the Sorbonne on Friday, who escaped from the van they'd been taken to, is an example to follow. When there are only three cops in a police van, we'll know what to do. The case of Sergeant Brunet, done over yesterday, will set a precedent: death to the pigs!

Already violence has shut the mouths of the petty bosses of the political groups; to challenge the bourgeois university alone is trivial when it's the whole of this society which is to be destroyed.

> LONG LIVE THE ZENGAKUREN!
> LONG LIVE THE VANDALIST COMMITTEE OF PUBLIC SAFETY (Bordeaux)
> LONG LIVE THE ENRAGÉS!
> LONG LIVE THE S.I.!
> LONG LIVE THE SOCIAL REVOLUTION!

The Enragés, Paris, May 6, 1968

THE CASTLE IS BURNING!

Address to the Council of the University of Paris

Relics of the past,

Your crass ignorance of life gives you no authority to do anything. Do you want proof? If you can sit today it will only be if you are backed up by a cordon of police. In fact nobody respects you any more. So cry now over your old Sorbonne.

It just makes me laugh that certain modernizing old farts are getting touchy about defending me, supposing — wrongly — that after having spat in their faces, I might once more become presentable enough for them to protect me. Despite their perseverance in such masochism, these opportunists wouldn't even know how to patch up the University. Monsieur Lefebvre, I say to you, shit.

There will be more and more of those who take from the education system the best thing it has: the grants. You've refused this to me, so I've had nothing to hide. I've got to bite the bullet.

Today's trial is, of course, a ridiculous fairy tale. The real trial took place on Monday on the streets, and secular justice has already detained about thirty rioters. For my comrades, what matters is the unconditional release of *all the prisoners* (as *well* as the students).

Freedom is the crime which contains all crimes. Woe betide feudal justice when the castle is burning!

René Riesel, Paris, May 10, 1968

UNTITLED TRACT PUBLISHED IN BORDEAUX IN APRIL, 1968:

The struggle against alienation must concern itself with giving words their true meaning, at the same time as conveying their elemental force:

So don't say:	Say instead:
society	racket
teacher	
psychologist	
poet	
sociologist	
militants (of all shades)	cops
conscientious objector	
trades unionist	
priest	
family	
(not a definitive list)	
news	distortions (as to the extent of the world racket and its mystifications)
work	hard labor
art	how much does that cost?
dialogue	masturbation
culture	shit gargled for ages by highbrowed cretins *(see: teacher)*
my sister	my love
teacher, sir	drop dead, you bastard!
goodnight father	drop dead, you bastard!
excuse me, officer	drop dead, you bastard!
thank you doctor	drop dead, you bastard!
legality	a trap for idiots

civilization	sterilization
town planning	preventative policing
village A,B,C,D	strategic hamlet
structuralism	the last chance for neo-capitalism, the outstanding failure of which is covered up by official lies clumsily plastered over the most flagrant contradictions

Students, you are impotent fools (we knew that already). But you'll remain so while you still haven't:

  – smashed your teachers' faces in;
  – buggered your priests;
  – fucking set fire to the faculty.

NO Nicholas, the Commune is not dead.[7]

Vandalist Committee of Public Safety

Section B:
The Enragés–S.I. Committee and the Council for the Maintenance of Occupations

COMMUNIQUÉ

Comrades,

Considering that the Sud-Aviation factory at Nantes has been occupied for two days by the workers and students of that city, and that today the movement is spreading to several factories (Nouvelles Messageries de la Presse Parisienne in Paris, Renault in Cleon, etc),

THE SORBONNE OCCUPATION COMMITTEE

calls for the immediate occupation of all the factories in France and the formation of workers' councils.

Comrades, spread and reproduce this appeal as quickly as possible.

Sorbonne, May 16, 1968, 3:30 P.M.

VIGILANCE!

Comrades,

The supremacy of the revolutionary assembly can only mean something if it exercises its power.

For the last 48 hours even the capacity of the general assembly to make decisions has been challenged by a systematic obstruction of all proposals for action.

Up until now no motion could be voted on or even discussed, and bodies elected by the general assembly (Occupation Committee and Coordinating Committee) see their work sabotaged by pseudo-spontaneous groups.

All the debates on organization, which people wanted to argue about before any action, are pointless if we do nothing.

AT THIS RATE, THE MOVEMENT WILL BE BURIED IN THE SORBONNE!

The prerequisite of direct democracy is the minimum support that revolutionary students can give to revolutionary workers who are occupying their factories.

It is inexcusable that yesterday evening's incidents in the GA should pass without retaliation.

The priests are holding us back when anti-clerical posters are torn up.

The bureaucrats are holding us back when, without even giving their names, they paralyze the revolutionary awareness that can take the movement forward from the barricades.

Once again, it's the future that is sacrificed to the re-establishment of the old unionism.

Parliamentary cretinism wants to take over the rostrum, as it tries to put the old, patched-up system back on its feet again.

Comrades,

The reform of the university alone is insignificant, when it is the whole of the old world which is to be destroyed.

The movement is nothing if it is not revolutionary.

Occupation Committee of the Sorbonne, May 16, 1968, 4:30 P.M.

WATCH OUT!

The Press Committee situated on the second floor, stair C, in the Gaston Azard library, represents only itself. It happens to be a case of a dozen or so student journalists anxious to prove themselves straight away to their future employers and future censors.

This Committee, which is trying to monopolize all contact with the Press, refuses to transmit the communiques of the regularly elected bodies of the general assembly.

THIS PRESS COMMITTEE IS A CENSORSHIP COMMITTEE: don't have anything more to do with it.

The various committees, commissions, working parties. can approach the AFP [French Press Agency] directly on 508-45-40 or the various newspapers:

Le Monde : 770 91 29

France-Soir : 508 28 00

Combat : leave a message with Robert Toubon, CEN 81 11.

The various working parties can, while waiting for this evening's general assembly where new decisions will be taken, address themselves to the occupation committee and the coordinating committee elected by the GA yesterday evening.

EVERYBODY COME TO THE GENERAL ASSEMBLY THIS EVENING IN ORDER TO THROW OUT THE BUREAUCRATS:

Occupation Committee of the autonomous and popular
The Sorbonne, May 16, 5 P.M.

WATCH OUT FOR MANIPULATORS!
WATCH OUT FOR BUREAUCRATS!

Comrades,

No-one must be unaware of the importance of the GA this evening [Thursday 16 May]. For two days individuals one recognizes from having seen them previously peddling their party lines have succeeded in sowing confusion and in smothering the GAs under a barrage of bureaucratic manipulations whose clumsiness clearly demonstrates the contempt they have for this assembly.

This assembly must learn to make itself respected, or disappear. Two points must be discussed above all:

—WHO IS IN CHARGE OF THE MARSHALS? whose disgusting role is intolerable.

—WHY IS THE PRESS COMMITTEE—which *dares to censor the communiques* that it is charged to transmit to the agencies—composed of apprentice journalists who are careful not to disappoint the ORTF bosses or jeopardize their future job possibilities?

Apart from this: as the workers are beginning to occupy several factories in France, FOLLOWING OUR EXAMPLE AND WITH THE SAME RIGHT WE HAVE, the Sorbonne occupation committee issued a statement approving of this movement at 3 P.M. this afternoon. The central problem of the present GA is therefore to declare itself by a clear vote supporting or disavowing this appeal of its occupation committee. In the case of a disavowal, this assembly will then have taken the responsibility of reserving for the students a right that it refuses to the working class; and in that case it is clear that it will no longer want to concern itself with anything but a Gaullist reform of the university.

Occupation Committee of the autonomous and popular Sorbonne University, 16
May 1968, 6:30 P.M.

SLOGANS TO BE SPREAD NOW BY EVERY MEANS

(Leaflets, announcements over microphones, comic strips, songs, graffiti, speech bubbles on paintings in the Sorbonne, announcements in theaters during films or while disrupting them, speech bubbles on subway billboards, before making love, after making love, in elevators, each time you raise your glass in a bar):

> OCCUPY THE FACTORIES
> ALL POWER TO THE WORKERS' COUNCILS
> ABOLISH CLASS SOCIETY
> DOWN WITH THE SPECTATOR COMMODITY SOCIETY
> ABOLISH ALIENATION
> END OF THE UNIVERSITY
> HUMANITY WILL ONLY BE HAPPY THE DAY THE LAST
>   BUREAUCRAT IS HUNG WITH THE GUTS OF THE LAST CAPITALIST
> DEATH TO THE COPS
> FREE ALSO THE 4 GUYS CONVICTED FOR LOOTING DURING 6 MAY
>
> *Occupation Committee of the autonomous and popular*
> *Sorbonne University, May 16, 1968, 7 P.M.*

MINIMUM DEFINITION OF REVOLUTIONARY ORGANIZATIONS

Since the only purpose of a revolutionary organization is the abolition of all existing classes in a way that does not bring about a new division of society, we consider any organization revolutionary which consistently and effectively works toward the international realization of the absolute power of the workers' councils, as prefigured in the experience of the proletarian revolutions of this century.

Such an organization makes a unitary critique of the world, or is nothing. By unitary critique we mean a comprehensive critique of all geographical areas where various forms of separate socioeconomic powers exist, as well as a comprehensive critique of all aspects of life.

Such an organization sees the beginning and end of its program in the complete decolonization of everyday life. It thus aims not at self-management by the masses of the existing world, but at its uninterrupted transformation. It embodies the radical critique of political economy, the supersession of the commodity and of wage labor.

Such an organization refuses to reproduce within itself any of the hierarchical conditions of the dominant world. The only limit to participating in its total democracy is that each member must have recognized and appropriated the coherence of its critique. This coherence must be both in the critical theory proper and in the relationship between this theory and practical activity. The organization radically criticizes every ideology as separate power of ideas and as ideas of separate power. It is thus at the same time the negation of any remnants of religion, and of the prevailing social spectacle which, from news media to mass culture, monopolizes communication between people around their unilateral reception of images of their alienated activity. The organization dissolves any "revolutionary ideology", unmasking it as a sign of the failure of the revolutionary project, as the private property of new specialists of power, as one more fraudulent representation settling itself above real proletarianized life.

Since the ultimate criterion of the modern revolutionary organization is its totality, such an organization is ultimately a critique of politics. It must explicitly aim to dissolve itself as a separate organization at its moment of victory.

Adopted by the 7th Conference of the S.I., July 1966

TEXTS OF SOME OF THE FIRST POSTERS
ON THE WALLS OF THE SORBONNE ON MAY 14, 1968

VIGILANCE!

The recuperators are amongst us!
"Annihilate as never before all that might one day destroy your work." (Sade)

Enragés-S.I. Committee

After God, art is dead. May its priests not bring it back again!
AGAINST any survival of art,
AGAINST the reign of separation,
DIRECT DIALOGUE
DIRECT ACTION
SELF-MANAGEMENT OF DAILY LIFE

Enragés-S.I. Committee

Comrades,
Let's dechristianize the Sorbonne immediately.
We can't tolerate a chapel here any longer!
Exhume the remains of the foul Richelieu, statesman and cardinal, and send them back to the Elysée and the Vatican.

Enragés-S.I. Committee

TEXTS OF TELEGRAMS SENT BY THE OCCUPATION COMMITTEE OF THE SORBONNE ON MAY 17, 1968

INTERNATIONAL INSTITUTE OF SOCIAL HISTORY AMSTERDAM NETHERLANDS / WE ARE CONSCIOUSLY STARTING TO CREATE OUR OWN HISTORY STOP WE ARE DETERMINED TO MAKE THIS KNOWN TO POSTERITY THROUGH YOUR INSTITUTE'S ARCHIVES STOP HUMANITY WILL ONLY BE HAPPY THE DAY THE LAST BUREAUCRAT IS HUNG WITH THE GUTS OF THE LAST CAPITALIST STOP LONG LIVE THE FACTORY OCCUPATIONS STOP LONG LIVE THE INTERNATIONAL POWER OF THE WORKERS' COUNCILS OCCUPATION COMMITTEE OF THE AUTONOMOUS AND POPULAR SORBONNE.

PROFESSOR IVAN SVITAK PRAGUE CZECHOSLOVAKIA / THE OCCUPATION COMMITTEE OF THE AUTONOMOUS AND POPULAR SORBONNE SENDS FRATERNAL SALUTATIONS TO COMRADE SVITAK AND TO CZECHOSLOVAKIAN REVOLUTIONARIES STOP LONG LIVE THE INTERNATIONAL POWER OF THE WORKERS' COUNCILS STOP HUMANITY WILL ONLY BE HAPPY THE DAY THE LAST BUREAUCRAT IS HUNG WITH THE GUTS OF THE LAST CAPITALIST STOP LONG LIVE REVOLUTIONARY MARXISM!

ZENGAKUREN TOKYO JAPAN / LONG LIVE THE STRUGGLE OF THE JAPANESE COMRADES WHO HAVE OPENED COMBAT SIMULTANEOUSLY ON THE FRONTS OF ANTI-STALINISM AND ANTI-IMPERIALISM STOP LONG LIVE THE FACTORY OCCUPATIONS STOP LONG LIVE THE GENERAL STRIKE STOP LONG LIVE THE INTERNATIONAL POWER OF THE WORKERS' COUNCILS STOP HUMANITY WILL ONLY BE HAPPY THE DAY THE LAST BUREAUCRAT IS HUNG WITH THE GUTS OF THE LAST CAPITALIST STOP OCCUPATION COMMITTEE OF THE AUTONOMOUS AND POPULAR SORBONNE

POLITBURO OF THE COMMUNIST PARTY OF THE USSR THE KREMLIN MOSCOW / SHAKE IN YOUR SHOES BUREAUCRATS STOP THE INTERNATIONAL POWER OF THE WORKERS' COUNCILS WILL SOON WIPE YOU OUT STOP HUMANITY WILL ONLY BE HAPPY THE DAY THE LAST BUREAUCRAT IS HUNG WITH THE GUTS OF THE LAST CAPITALIST STOP LONG LIVE THE STRUGGLE OF THE KRONSTADT SAILORS AND OF THE MAKHNOVSHCHINA AGAINST TROTSKY AND LENIN STOP LONG LIVE THE 1956 COUNCILIST INSURRECTION OF BUDAPEST STOP DOWN WITH THE STATE STOP LONG LIVE REVOLUTIONARY MARXISM STOP OCCUPATION COMMITTEE OF THE AUTONOMOUS AND POPULAR SORBONNE

POLITBURO OF THE CHINESE COMMUNIST PARTY GATE OF CELESTIAL PEACE PEKING / SHAKE IN YOUR SHOES BUREAUCRATS STOP THE INTERNATIONAL POWER OF THE WORKERS' COUNCILS WILL SOON WIPE YOU OUT STOP HUMANITY WILL ONLY BE HAPPY THE DAY THE LAST BUREAUCRAT IS HUNG WITH THE GUTS OF THE LAST CAPITALIST STOP LONG LIVE THE FACTORY OCCUPATIONS STOP LONG LIVE THE GREAT CHINESE PROLETARIAN REVOLUTION OF 1927 BETRAYED BY THE STALINIST BUREAUCRATS STOP LONG LIVE THE PROLETARIANS OF CANTON AND ELSEWHERE WHO HAVE TAKEN UP ARMS AGAINST THE SO-CALLED PEOPLE'S ARMY STOP LONG LIVE THE CHINESE WORKERS AND STUDENTS WHO HAVE ATTACKED THE SO-CALLED CULTURAL REVOLUTION AND THE MAOIST BUREAUCRATIC ORDER STOP LONG LIVE REVOLUTIONARY MARXISM STOP DOWN WITH THE STATE STOP OCCUPATION COMMITTEE OF THE AUTONOMOUS AND POPULAR SORBONNE

REPORT ON THE OCCUPATION OF THE SORBONNE

The occupation of the Sorbonne that began Monday 13 May has inaugurated a new period in the crisis of modern society. The events now taking place in France foreshadow the return of the proletarian revolutionary movement in all countries. The movement that had already advanced from theory to struggle in the streets has now advanced to a struggle for power over the means of production. Modernized capitalism thought it had finished with class struggle — but it's started up again! The proletariat no longer existed — but here it is again.

In surrendering the Sorbonne, the government counted on pacifying the student revolt, which had already succeeded in holding a section of Paris behind its barricades an entire night, before it was recaptured with great difficulty by the police. The Sorbonne was given over to the students in the hope that they would peacefully discuss their university problems. But the occupiers immediately decided to open it to the public, freely to discuss the general problems of society. This was thus a prefiguration of a *council,* a council in which even the students broke out of their miserable studenthood and ceased to be students.

To be sure, the occupation has never been total: a chapel and some remnants of administrative offices have been tolerated. Democracy has never been complete: future technocrats of the UNEF claimed to be making themselves useful, and other political bureaucrats have also tried their manipulations. Workers' participation has remained very limited and the presence of non-students soon began to be questioned. Many students, professors, journalists, and imbeciles of other occupations have come as spectators.

In spite of all these deficiencies, which are not surprising considering the contradiction between the scope of the project and the narrowness of the student milieu, the exemplary nature of the best aspects of this situation immediately took on an explosive significance. Workers could not fail to be inspired by seeing free discussion, the striving for a radical critique and direct democracy in action. Even limited to a Sorbonne liberated from the state, this was a revolutionary program developing its own forms. The day after the occupation of the Sorbonne the Sud-Aviation workers of Nantes occupied their factory. On the third day, Thursday 16th, the Renault factories at Cleon and Flins were occupied and the movement began at the NMPP and at Boulogne-Billancourt, starting at Shop 70. Now, at the end of the week, one hundred factories have been occupied, while the waves of strikes, accepted but never initiated by the union bureaucracies, are paralyzing the railroads and developing towards a general strike.

The only power in the Sorbonne was the general assembly of its occupiers. At its first session, on 14 May, amidst a certain confusion, it had elected an "occupation committee" of fifteen members revocable by it each day. Only one of the delegates, belonging to the Nanterre-Paris Enragés group, had set forth a program: defense of direct democracy in the Sorbonne and absolute power of workers' councils as the ultimate goal. The next day's general assembly reelected its entire Occupation

Committee, which had not been able to accomplish anything by then. In fact, all the specialized groupings that had set themselves up in the Sorbonne followed the directives of a hidden "coordination committee" composed of volunteer and very moderating organizers responsible to no-one. An hour after the reelection of the occupation committee one of the "coordinators" privately tried to declare it dissolved. A direct appeal to the rank and file in the courtyard of the Sorbonne aroused a movement of protests which obliged the manipulator to retract himself. By the next day, Thursday 16th, thirteen members of the occupation committee had disappeared, leaving two comrades, including the Enrages member, vested with the only delegation of power authorized by the general assembly – this at a time when the gravity of the moment necessitated immediate decisions: democracy was constantly being flouted in the Sorbonne and factory occupations were spreading. The occupation committee, rallying round it as many Sorbonne occupiers as it could who were determined to maintain democracy there, at 3 P.M. launched an appeal for "the occupation of all the factories in France and the formation of workers' councils". To disseminate this appeal, the occupation committee had at the same time to restore the democratic functioning of the Sorbonne. It had to take over or recreate from scratch all the services that were supposed to be under its authority: the loudspeaker system, printing facilities, interfaculty liaison, security. It ignored the squawking complaints of the spokesmen of various political groups (JCR, Maoists, etc.), reminding them that it was responsible only to the general assembly. It intended to report to it that very evening, but the Sorbonne occupiers' unanimous decision to march on Renault-Billancourt (whose occupation we had learned of in the meantime) postponed the session of the assembly until 2 P.M. the next day.

During the night, while thousands of comrades were at Billancourt, some unidentified persons improvised a general assembly, which broke up when the occupation committee, having learned of its existence, sent back two delegates to call attention to its illegitimacy.

Friday the 17th at 2 P.M. the regular assembly saw its rostrum occupied for a long time by self-appointed marshals belonging to the FER; and in addition had to interrupt the session for the second march on Billancourt at 5 P.M.

That evening at 9 P.M. the occupation committee was finally able to present a report of its activities. It was completely unsuccessful, however, in getting its actions discussed and voted on, in particular its appeal for the occupation of the factories, which the assembly did not take the responsibility of either disavowing or approving. Confronted with such indifference and confusion, the occupation committee had no choice but to withdraw. The assembly showed itself just as incapable of protesting against a new invasion of the rostrum by the FER troops, whose putsch seemed to be aimed at countering the provisional alliance of the JCR and UNEF bureaucrats. The partisans of direct democracy immediately declared that they no longer had anything to do at the Sorbonne.

At the very moment when the example of the occupation is beginning to be taken up in the factories it is collapsing at the Sorbonne. This is all the more serious since the workers have against them a bureaucracy infinitely more entrenched than that of the student or leftist amateurs. In addition, the leftist bureaucrats, echoing the CGT in the hope of being accorded a little marginal role alongside it, abstractly separate the workers from the students, whom "they don't need lessons from." But in fact the students have already given a lesson to the workers precisely by occupying the Sorbonne and briefly initiating a really democratic discussion. All the bureaucrats tell us demogogically that the working class is grown up, in order to hide the fact that it is enchained – first of all by them (now or in their future hopes, depending on which group they're in). They counterpoise their lying seriousness to "the festival" in the Sorbonne, but it was precisely this festiveness that bore within itself the only thing that is serious: the radical critique of prevailing conditions.

The student struggle is now left behind. Even more left behind are all the second string bureaucratic leaderships that think it's a good idea to feign respect for the Stalinists at this very moment when the CGT and the so-called "Communist" Party are *trembling*. The outcome of the present crisis is in the hands of the workers themselves if they succeed in accomplishing in the occupation of their factories the goals toward which the university occupation was only able to make a rough gesture.

The comrades who supported the first Sorbonne occupation committee – the Enragés–Situationist International Committee, a number of workers and a few students – have formed a Council for the Maintenance of Occupations: the maintaining of the occupations obviously being conceivable only through their quantitative and qualitative extension, which must not spare any existing regime.

Council for the Maintenance of Occupations, Paris, May 19, 1968

FOR THE POWER OF THE WORKERS' COUNCILS

In the space of ten days workers have occupied hundreds of factories, a spontaneous general strike has totally interrupted the activity of the country, and *de facto* committees have taken over many buildings belonging to the state. In such a situation – which in any event cannot last but must either extend itself or disappear (through repression or defeatist negotiations) – all the old ideas are swept aside and all the radical hypotheses on the return of the revolutionary proletarian movement are confirmed. The fact that the whole movement was really triggered five months ago by a half dozen revolutionaries of the "Enragés" group reveals even better how much the objective conditions were already present. At this very moment the French example is having repercussions in other countries and reviving the internationalism which is part and parcel of the revolutions of our century.

The fundamental struggle today is between, on the one hand, the mass of workers – who do not have direct means of expressing themselves – and on the other, the leftist political and union bureaucracies that (even if merely on the basis of the 14% of the active population that is unionized) control the factory gates and the right to negotiate in the name of the occupiers. These bureaucracies are not workers' organizations that have degenerated and betrayed the workers, they are a mechanism for integrating the workers into capitalist society. In the present crisis they are the main protection of this shaken capitalism.

The de Gaulle regime may negotiate — essentially (if only indirectly) with the PCF–CGT — for the demobilization of the workers in exchange for some economic advantages; after which the radical currents would be repressed. Or "the left" may come to power and pursue the same policies, though from a weaker position. Or an armed repression may be attempted. Or finally, the workers may take the upper hand by speaking for themselves and becoming conscious of goals as radical as the forms of struggle they have already put into practice. Such a process would lead to the formation of workers' councils making decisions democratically at the rank and file level, federating with each other by means of delegates revocable at any moment, and becoming the sole deliberative and executive power over the entire country.

In what way could the prolongation of the present situation lead to such a prospect? Within a few days, perhaps, the necessity of starting certain sectors of the economy back up again under workers' control could lay the bases for this new power, a power which everything is already pushing to burst through the constraints of the unions and parties. The railroads and print shops would have to be put back into operation for the needs of the workers' struggle. New *de facto* authorities would have to requisition and distribute food. If money became devalued it might have to be replaced by vouchers backed by those new authorities. It is through such a practical process that the consciousness of the profound will of the proletariat can impose itself — the class consciousness that lays hold on history and brings about the workers' domination over all aspects of their own lives.

Council for the Maintenance of Occupations, Paris, May 22, 1968

ADDRESS TO ALL WORKERS

Comrades,
What we have already done in France is haunting Europe and will soon threaten all the ruling classes of the world, from the bureaucrats of Moscow and Peking to the millionaires of Washington and Tokyo. *Just as we have made Paris dance*, the international proletariat will again take up its assault on the capitals of all states, on all the citadels of alienation. The occupation of factories and public buildings throughout the country has not only blocked the functioning of the economy, it has brought about a general questioning of society. A deep-seated movement is leading almost every sector of the population to seek a real change of life. It is now a revolutionary movement, a movement which lacks nothing but the *consciousness of what it has already done* in order to triumph.

What forces will try to save capitalism? The regime will fall unless it threatens recourse to arms (accompanied by the promise of new elections, which could only take place after the capitulation of the movement) or even resorts to immediate armed repression. As for the possible coming to power of the left, it too will try to defend the old world through concessions and through force. In this event, the best defender of such a "popular government" would be the so-called "Communist" Party, the party of Stalinist bureaucrats, which has fought the movement from the very beginning and which began to envisage the fall of the de Gaulle regime only when it realized it was no longer capable of being that regime's main guardian. Such a transitional government would really be "Kerenskyist" only if the Stalinists were beaten. All this will depend essentially on the workers' consciousness and capacity for autonomous organization: those who have already rejected the ridiculous agreement that so gratified the union leaders need only discover that they cannot "win" much more within the framework of the existing economy, but that they can take everything by transforming all the bases of the economy on their own behalf. The bosses can hardly pay more; but they can disappear.

The present movement did not become "politicized" by going beyond the miserable union demands regarding wages and pensions, demands which were falsely presented as "social questions." It is beyond *politics*: it is posing *the social question* in its simple truth. The revolution that has been in the making for over a century is returning. It can assert itself only in its own forms. It is already too late for a bureaucratic-revolutionary patching up. When a recently destalinized Andre Baronet calls for the formation of a common organization that would bring together "all the authentic forces of revolution... whether they march under the banner of Trotsky or Mao, of anarchy or situationism," we have only to recall that those who today follow Trotsky or Mao, to say nothing of the pitiful "Anarchist Federation," have nothing to do with the present revolution. The bureaucrats may now change their minds about what they call "authentically revolutionary"; authentic revolution does not have to change its condemnation of bureaucracy.

At the present moment, with the power they hold and with the parties and unions being what they are, the workers have no other choice but to organize themselves in unitary rank and file committees directly seizing all aspects of the reconstruction of social life, asserting their autonomy *vis-à-vis* any sort of politico-unionist leadership, ensuring their self-defense and federating with each other regionally and nationally. By taking this path they will become the sole real power in the country, the power of the *Workers' Councils*. Otherwise the proletariat, because it is "either revolutionary or nothing," will again become a passive object. It will go back to watching television.

What defines the power of the councils? Dissolution of all external power, direct and total democracy; practical unification of decision and execution; delegates who can be revoked at any moment by those who have mandated them; abolition of hierarchy and independent specializations; conscious management and transformation of all the conditions of liberated life; permanent creative participation of the masses; internationalist extension and coordination. The present requirements are nothing less than this. Self-management is nothing less. Beware of *the recuperators* of every modernist variety — including even priests — who are beginning to talk of self-management or even of workers' councils without acknowledging this *minimum*, because they in fact want to save their bureaucratic functions, the privileges of their intellectual specializations, or their future as petty bosses!

In reality what is necessary now has been necessary since the beginning of the proletarian revolutionary project. People struggled for the abolition of wage labor, of commodity production, of the state. It was a matter of acceding to conscious history, of suppressing all separations and "everything that exists independently of individuals." Proletarian revolution has spontaneously sketched out its appropriate form in the councils, in Saint Petersburg in 1905 as in Turin in 1920, in Catalonia in 1936 as in Budapest in 1956. The maintaining of the old society, or the formation of new exploiting classes, has each time been by way of the suppression of the councils. Now the working class knows its enemies and its own appropriate methods of action. "Revolutionary organization has had to learn that it can no longer *fight alienation with alienated forms*" (*The Society of the Spectacle*). Workers' councils are clearly the only solution, since all the other forms of revolutionary struggle have led to the opposite of what was aimed at.

Enragés–S.I. Committee
Council for the Maintenance of Occupations, May 30, 1968

THE COMMUNE'S NOT DEAD

(Written in June 1968, to be sung to the tune of "The Song of Eugene Poitier.")

> At the barricades of Gay-Lussac,
> The Enragés at our head,
> We unleashed the attack:
> Oh bloody hell, what a party!
> We were in ecstasy amongst the cobblestones
> Seeing the old world go up in flames.
>
> CHORUS: All that has shown, Carmela,
> That the Commune's not dead (repeat)
>
> To brighten things up, the combatants,
> Fucking set fire to the cars:
> One match and, Forward!
> Poetry written in petrol.
> And you should have seen the CRS
> Really get their asses burnt!
>
> (chorus)

Politicized, the *blousons noirs*,
Seized the Sorbonne,
To help them fight and destroy,
They put no faith in anybody.
Theory was realized,
The shops were looted

(chorus)

What you produce belongs to you,
It's the bosses who are the thieves.
They are taking the piss out of you,
When they make you pay in the shops.
While waiting for self-management,
We'll apply the critique of the brick.

(chorus)

All the parties, the unions,
And their bureaucrats,
Oppress the proletariat,
As much as the bourgeoisie.
Against the state and its allies,
Let's form workers' councils.

(chorus)

The Occupation Committee,
Spits on Trotskyists,
Maoists and other prats,
Who exploit the strikers.
Next time there'll be blood spilt,
By the enemies of freedom.

(chorus)

Now that the insurgents
Have gone back to survival.
Boredom, forced labor,
And ideologies,
We'll take pleasure in sowing
Other May flowers to be picked one day.

FINAL CHORUS: All that has shown, Carmela.
That the Commune's not dead (repeat)

SONG OF THE COUNCIL FOR THE MAINTENANCE OF OCCUPATIONS

(To the tune of "Our Soldiers at La Rochelle" sung by Jacques Donai.)

In Rue Gay-Lussac, the rebels
Have only the cars to burn.
What would you want then, my love?
What is it then you'd want?

CHORUS: Guns. by the hundred.
Rifles by the thousand.
Guns and rifles by the thousand.

Tell me what's the name
Of the game that you're playing?
The rules seem to be new;
What a game, what an unusual game!

(chorus)

The revolution, my love
Is the game that you're talking about.
It's played in the back alleys.
It's played thanks to the paving stones.

(chorus)

The old world and all its crew,
We want to sweep away.
We've got to be cruel:
Death to the cops and the priests.

(chorus)

Against us they fire a hail
Of grenades and CS gas.
We've only got shovels
And knives to arm ourselves with.

(chorus)

My poor children, says she,
My fine barricaders,

My heart, my heart flutters.
I have nothing to give you.

(chorus)

If I have faith in my fight.
I need not fear the police.
But must make common cause
With our comrades the workers.

(chorus)

Gaullism is a fuck up
No one can doubt that any more.
Bureaucrats into the dustbin:
Without them we could have won.

(chorus)

In Rue Gay-Lussac, the rebels
Have only the cars to burn.
What would you want then, my love?
What is it then you'd want

(chorus)

Section C: Other documents

SORBONNE ANTI-GAS LEAFLET

22 March Movement 22 March Movement 22 March Movement

Anti-Gas Measures

1 *Preventative measures*
   —If you have no gas mask, underwater, motorcycle or ski goggles, etc. (close fitting): keep a half lemon in the mouth (to aid respiration), and some cotton around the nose and mouth.

—*Don't* stay in a layer of gas, wet the material around your mouth, open water faucets, put water in your eyes or face because it may react with the gas to give off toxic products.

—Don't breathe the gas from offensive grenades (the ones which make a lot of noise going off).

—On the skin: a layer of make-up base or vaseline.

—For the eyes: drops, except HYDROCORTISONE OR OTHER CORTISONE DROPS.

2 If someone is overcome by fumes:

Not all doctors know what to do.

A 1 Get the patient, without letting him make any effort, to a heated, well-ventilated room

2 Be sure that he moves as little as possible

3 Apply a drop of sulphurated ether to the nostrils.

B Let the patient get as much oxygen as possible and leave him to rest.

C No food or drink for *four hours* after absorbing the gas.

—With serious cases, there is a risk of dry pulmonary lesions (bronchitis, spitting up blood) or in the case of saturation - death by pulmonary lesions.

—Chlorine grenades (in transparent plastic cylinders) are corrosive and attack the external and internal mucous membranes.

TO PROTECT AGAINST PROJECTILES . . .

—Don't wear any nylon clothing (which burns), nor paper wadding.

—Do wear a crash helmet if possible, or construction worker's hat.

—If a grenade falls near you, do not pick it up. Move away. It may explode.

For blood donors: the National Blood Transfusion Centre, or any of the local centers.

HERE AT THE HEART OF CONDONING OF INTELLIGENCE... WHERE ARE YOU, COMRADES?

In Paris, tearing off the organizational shackles of the old world, revolutionary violence has been let loose in the streets: agitation, street-fighting, barricades, students rebelling inside the cop vans.

In Bordeaux, you're just living on the level of the "Parisian–student" spectacle.

Revolutionary false consciousness is characterized by the level of its alienation bathed in the sun of the ideological spectacle (when consciousness decays, ideology oozes out) — it mystifies the gift of its own life while giving itself up to the highest bidder.

The exemplary passivity consciously developed by the bureaucratic apparatus only develops contemplation and self-satisfaction in exchange for leaders. It only succeeds in laying pseudo-acts over pseudo-events under the cover of pseudo-discussions.

Your demonstrations were no more than strolls. Your occupation was no more than a preoccupation. Every creative act on the subjective level, even the most feeble, is perceived as disturbing. The vast spectacular edifice which has been built up at Pessac University.

Settle your own affairs yourselves!

It's not only this university which is for the chop, it's the whole of consumer society.

Your turn to play comrades...

Committee for the Maintenance of Occupations (Bordeaux)

UNTITLED APPEAL IN FRENCH AND ARABIC, PARIS, MAY 22, 1968

We North African workers, aware of the importance of the fight conducted by the French workers and students,

despite the inherent difficulties in our position as immigrants,

despite the threats of expulsion that hang over us,

despite the super-exploitation that we are subjected to and the precariousness of our situation,

must, without hesitation, stand up for the fight conducted in France by the students and workers.

Our participation in the strike is our only way of proving we're not commodities to be used as a means of blackmailing the French proletariat, the only way of proving that proletarian internationalism is our watchword.

The struggle that we are conducting (and which we'll carry on to the end) with the French proletariat, is our struggle. In fact our aim is the destruction of monopoly capitalism and, its extension in our own countries, imperialism.

We know that capitalism is the best supporter and ally of the police and military dictatorships which exploit us in the guise of nationalism or pseudo-socialism.

The mortal blow which the French proletariat will deliver to capitalism and imperialism will be a first step towards the destruction of the dictatorships which we in our own countries, and our brothers in the Third World, are victim to:

- confined in slums;
- reduced to poverty wages;
- prisoners of police and governmental repression;
- targets of racism from all sides;
- slaves of the employers;
- forced to emigrate.

We North African workers have chosen the Revolution.

We salute the revolutionary assault which is shaking the arthritic structures of capitalism in order to replace it with the direct power of the workers. The victory of the French proletariat is our victory.

Our support and solidarity are a step towards the Revolution in our own countries.

Long live the Socialist Revolution!
Long live Self-management!
Down with the reactionary police states in Tunisia and Morocco!
Down with the military-bureaucratic dictatorship in Algeria!

North African Action Committee

MEDICINE AND REPRESSION

It is not an "accident" that has awoken the depoliticized consumer, an accident whose cause would be the brutality of the police. Just as the student revolt cannot be reduced to the fanaticism of "a few Enrages," the police repression cannot be reduced to the sadism of a few "cops" and to the "stupidity" of their bosses; and in neither case is it any longer a question of an isolated fact, a temporary and inconsequential aberration of our harmonious civilization.

On the contrary this civilization is the habitual disguise that permanent repression adopts in order to conceal and perpetuate itself. Because normally this repression doesn't adopt the tell-tale, crystal clear image of the helmeted policeman, but rather the less shocking, better accepted (often even desirable) uniforms such as the doctor's white coat or the teacher's black gown.

Instead of shedding tears over the injured (for the injuries denote what should be for us a lesson in courage) it would be better for example to concern ourselves with Roche's blunders,[8] which allowed us to live so intensely the fact that the police and university have the same function: to uphold and reproduce bourgeois order.

The health service shares with the two former agencies and a few others (e.g. the judicial system) the role of cementing over and filling in the cracks which might appear in our social structure. The repressive and yet flexible function of the health service which we wish to reveal here can be shown at its three levels of organization.

I. The social avocation of health care

The doctor thinks of himself as the boss when he's only the foreman. The permission to "touch" the sick that he grants in such niggardly fashion to other health workers, like so many scraps of his "power," are the gold stars which he dispenses to reward the good behaviour of his "subordinates." The limits of this permission are the prohibitions that the doctor gives out like so many diktats, and in which he bases his justification for a knowledge of which he is the sole source.

Why, for example, justify the demarcation between the intramuscular injection and the intravenous injection, which marks the limits of the nurses' power? Because the doctor, in order to hide the lack of scientific foundation for his art has to set up arbitrary distinctions — otherwise this lack of scientific foundation would reveal the ideological nature of medical knowledge and its submission to the dominant ideology, i.e. bourgeois ideology.

From this constraint (which makes it impossible for the doctor radically to criticize his method and his ends, in other words quite simply restricting his freedom to think) the ideological system compensates him, as opposed to other health workers, by binding him to the bourgeois class and giving him the illusion that he alone holds therapeutic power; thus obliging him to be the guardian of this ideology.

II. The content and organization of medical studies

Medical studies only carry fragmentary knowledge: studies of the sick body and the healthy body, cut off from humanity in two essential dimensions: social human being and the human being subject to desires (excluding the human sciences and half excluding psychology).

Such studies develop under the form, not of a critical apprenticeship, but of an acquisition through memory of a pseudo-science which only finds its material by a confused recourse to concepts from other sciences, and which lose all coherence in this transfer.

The importance accorded to the presence in the hospital, and above all the mode of integration, of the student is revealing: straight away the student endorses the doctor's status, he is called "Doctor" from the first day, henceforth the student is only able to reach out towards this mythical image: all possibility of criticism or confrontation is taken away from him, just as it is impossible to put into question his mode of relations with his future "subordinates,"

The fundamental institution of medical studies is based in any case on the EXAMINATION, the function of which is to synthesize this acquisition of this pseudo-knowledge and mythical status.

III. Society's methods of taking care of illness
and the place that they assign to the doctor

It appears that one of the roles of the Faculty of Medicine is to prepare the students for their real task: from biological concepts, it molds doctors into the service of capitalist oppression insofar as it forbids them to oppose illness in its socio-economic dimension.

Capitalist society, under the cover of an apparent neutrality (liberalism, medical vocation, peaceful humanism) puts the doctor side by side with the forces of oppression: he is charged with keeping the population fit both for work and consumption (e.g. the doctor who checks fitness to work). The doctor is charged with making people accept a society which makes them ill (e.g. psychiatry).

Although the doctor's independence may be proclaimed and defended by the ranks of doctors... (who don't say a word until the forces of order oppose the collection and treatment of the injured) — this independence is massively reduced by the fact that the doctor is charged not only with struggling against illness, but with taking care of it to the exclusion of social life. A real struggle against illness, implying a considerable extension of the idea of preventative medicine, would rapidly become political and revolutionary, as it would be a struggle against an inhibitory and repressive society.

National Young Doctors' Center, 13 rue Pascal, Paris V.

COMMUNIQUE OF MAY 7, 1968

The CNJM[9] declares itself in solidarity with the struggles led in France by the student movement for:

—a free discussion in the heart of the university on education and the ideology which supports it;

— a questioning of the pedagogic relationship and the socioeconomic ends of the university;

The CNJM states in particular that present day medical education aims at molding doctors into a role whose aim is to make people accept a society which makes them ill.

The CNJM is delighted to see the formation, from one county to another, of a movement of universal confrontation of unprecedented depth.

The CNJM protests against the police repression which has been unleashed on the students at the instigation of Power, and with the complicity of the most reactionary elements in the university.

EVERYTHING IS POSSIBLE WITH THE ACTIVE STRENGTH OF THE WORKING CLASS

The movement of strikes and occupations following on from the night of 10-11 May, must lead to the accomplishment of the historical goals of the proletariat (goals which have since become immediate), or it will be finished off through a compromise with capitalist power, terms of which will find the proletariat once more a slave of Capital.

Remember June '36: "One must know how to end a strike" (Thorez) [Communist Party leader], and to get the workers to leave the factories a 40 hour week was conceded, which led to unbridled exploitation through basic rate pay, piecework, bonuses, time keeping and overtime.

The present factory occupations must continue to extend themselves throughout the economic system, the banks included. But this occupation must take the form of the "restitution of the instruments of production to Society" (K. Marx).

Now this restitution can only be made by the intervention of the workers themselves. So it's not a case of giving the factories and faculties back to Capital in exchange for a few concessions, however important, but of keeping them as COMMUNIST PROPERTY AND PUTTING THEM IN GEAR, along with the rest of the social and economic mechanism—production, consumption, education etc. — in the service of humanity, without exploitation.

Those who envisage a compromise with Capital and its state are betraying the working class.

Two apparently important concessions could be made by the government right away: nationalization of the key industries, and the joint-management of enterprises — in other words, an acceptance of a few workers supervising the exploitation of the proletariat as a whole; and so much the better if they are "democratically" elected like members of parliament.

NO TO THE JOINT MANAGEMENT OF BUSINESSES. WORKERS MUST EXERCISE EXCLUSIVE CONTROL OVER THE WHOLE ECONOMY AND OVER POLITICAL POWER.

NO TO THE NATIONALIZATIONS THAT POWER WOULD BE READY TO CONCEDE UNDER THE GUISE OF SOCIALISM. Besides the fact that this would install a state capitalism, it would do nothing to alleviate the lot of the workers (for instance, Renault, etc.).

The working class, if united by revolutionary ideas and not behind capitulators, is strong enough to assert itself, and to do so almost without violence. If all the workers and students of France took such a revolutionary stance, all the repressive institutions of the capitalist state would be rendered useless and wither away.

It's in order to hinder such a socialist development that the unions and their parties talk about eliminating any interference that comes from outside the working class (an allusion to the students' show of solidarity), and of doing nothing that has not been democratically decided on in their union meetings.

Revolutionary democracy, which begins with the ABSOLUTE sovereignty of the working class, over and above all parties and unions WHICHEVER THEY MAY BE, is far superior to the parties and unions who dare to say to the working class: keep the factories only until the new forms of exploitation are agreed on (new collective bargaining).

These are the same people who put the working class on guard against outside interference. In reality where does outside interference come from? The law forbids the election of delegates not approved of by the unions, a great privilege granted by the capitalist state to its agents detached inside the working class. And this is why the CGT resolution (in *L'Humanité*, May 18) urges the extension of union freedom, now opposed to the freedom of the workers.

WORKERS! APPOINT YOUR OWN DELEGATES AND YOUR OWN FACTORY COMMITTEES (SOVIETS) INDEPENDENTLY OF ALL UNION AND POLITICAL AFFILIATIONS.

WELCOME REPRESENTATIVES FROM OTHER WORKING CLASS COMMUNITIES, STUDENTS, AND WAGE WORKERS IN GENERAL.

Those who are afraid of the present struggle are the ones who wish to keep the privileges which the law has granted them.

The CGT pretends It is the working class, just like de Gaulle pretends that He is France. Now it's a fact that the Gaullist state relies on the CGT and the other main unions, even subsidizing them, making them organs of the system of exploitation and therefore forces from outside the proletariat, in other words, the enemy.

THE FUTURE OF THE PRESENT MOVEMENT DEPENDS ON FREE DISCUSSION AT THE HEART OF THOSE BODIES ELECTED BY THE WORKING CLASS IN ITS ENTIRETY.

FORWARD TO A COMMUNIST SOCIETY WITHOUT CAPITAL OR WAGED WORK!

10 May Group—World Revolution, Paris, May 19, 1968

FOOTBALL TO THE FOOTBALLERS!

We footballers belonging to various clubs in the Paris region have today decided to occupy the headquarters of the French Football Federation. Just like the workers are occupying their factories, and the students occupying their faculties. *Why?*

IN ORDER TO GIVE BACK TO THE 600,000 FRENCH FOOTBALLERS AND TO THEIR THOUSANDS OF FRIENDS WHAT BELONGS TO THEM: FOOTBALL. WHICH THE PONTIFFS OF THE FEDERATION HAVE EXPROPRIATED FROM THEM IN ORDER TO SERVE THEIR EGOTISTICAL INTERESTS AS SPORTS PROFITEERS.

By the terms of Article 1 of the Rules of the Federation (according to the law a non profit-making Association), the pontiffs of the Federation are engaged in working for the "development of football." We accuse them of having worked against football and of having accelerated its decline by submitting it to the tutelage of a government that is by its very nature hostile to popular sport.

1st THEY HAVE ACCEPTED AN EIGHT MONTH LIMITATION TO THE FOOTBALL SEASON and have forbidden it at the best time of the year, while turning a blind eye to the closure of the grounds, the refusal of collective travel arrangements, and the refusal of accident insurance guarantees during the "forbidden" period.

2nd THEY HAVE DONE NOTHING TO PREVENT THE CLOSURE OF NUMEROUS FOOTBALL GROUNDS or help create new ones. Which makes it impossible for hundreds of thousands of young people to practice their sport. Neither have they done anything to allow schoolchildren to play football indoors.

3rd THEY ARE GOING TO CREATE THE LICENSE B, which, by practically forbidding transfers (except when it's in the interests of the big clubs), constitutes an intolerable affront to the freedom of the players and the interests of the smaller clubs.

4th THROUGH THE VOICE OF DUGAUGUEZ, THEY HAVE INSULTED ALL FRENCH FOOTBALLERS regarding their physical, technical, and mental abilities.

5th THEY SCOFF AT THE HUMAN DIGNITY OF THE BEST FOOTBALLERS AMONG US, the professionals, by maintaining the slavish contract denounced by Kopa, the illegality of which was recognized a year ago by Sadoul, President of the Board of Directors.

6th THEY SHAMELESSLY CONCENTRATE IN THE HANDS OF A FEEBLE MINORITY THE SUBSTANTIAL PROFITS that we procure for them through our subscriptions, and by the receipts from which they deduct percentages in advance, if they don't take the whole lot. Chiarisoli, President of the Federation and Sadoul, President of the Board, dish out illegal appointments under the budgetary headings that escape the control of the players. Boulogne, head of the trainers' Mafia keeps the most lucrative posts for his friends (one million francs or more per month). Dugauguez asserts himself as the full-time manager of the French national team (600,000 francs a month) yet has kept his positions as business manager of Sedan Draperies and trainer of Sedan. And to cap it all there is Pierre Delaunay who owes his post as General Secretary of the Federation to heredity (like a little Louis XVI), because he was nominated to the title by his father, previous holder of this office!

It's to put an end to these incredible practices that we are occupying the property of the 600,000 French footballers, which has become the bastion of the enemies and exploiters of football.

Now it's up to you: footballers, trainers, managers of small clubs, countless friends and fans of football, students and workers – to preserve the quality of your sport by joining us to: DEMAND AN END to the arbitrary limitation of the football season; to the License B to the slavish contract of the professional players.

DEMAND THE IMMEDIATE DISMISSAL (by means of a referendum of the 600,000 footballers, controlled by themselves) of the profiteers of football and the insulters of the footballers.

FREE FOOTBALL FROM THE TUTELAGE OF THE MONEY OF THE PATHETIC PRETEND-PATRONS who are at the root of the decay of football. And demand from the state the SUBSIDIES that it accords to all the other sports, and which the pontiffs of the Federation have never claimed.

So that football may remain yours, we call on you to MAKE YOUR WAY WITHOUT DELAY to the headquarters of the Federation which has again become YOUR HOUSE, at 60 Avenue d'lena, Paris.

United, we will make football once again what it ought never to have ceased to be – the sport of joy, the sport of the world of tomorrow which all the workers have started building. EVERYONE TO 60 AVENUE D'IENA!

Footballers' Action Committee

CENSIER ACTION COMMITTEE LEAFLET

Millions of workers are on strike.

They are occupying their places of work in the same way that the students began occupying their faculties.

Don't let any one person make the decisions for all. The action committees are there for that.

The action committee is the rank and file organization of all those who wish to act, whatever their old political or union allegiances – which today have been superseded.

–Only the spontaneity of the workers as a whole will allow the most radical results to be obtained, that no chapel, no old organization, no party, and no new boss can exploit for their own personal advantage.

–It is the power of the working class that needs to be organized. At the present time, the action committees are the appropriate instruments to deal with this.

–The ACs must, on terrain chosen by them, seize their objective and realize it immediately, becoming EVERYTHING THAT THE OTHER ORGANIZATIONS ARE NOT.

–The masses have got nothing to hide, and they have a right to know all. Truth alone is revolutionary. So act on their level, in such a way that the least demands should be known by all, and be put forward with the same importance as any other.

In this way the *totality* of demands will appear, and their incalculable number will produce the evidence that the capitalist regime cannot really satisfy the least of them.

It's not a case of demanding more of this or more of that. It's a case of demanding something else altogether. For its part, the Censier AC organizes:

  —collections to help striker – money, food, etc.;
  —meetings in the factories;
  —leaflet distribution from many locations.

The Censier AC calls for:

  —a tenants' strike;
  —a transport strike;
  —a tax strike.

It proposes:

  —the occupation of empty flats;
  —the organization of goods in the supermarkets and their free distribution to strikers and their families;
  —the immediate disbandment of the forces of repression, CRS etc., and the disarming of the police.

The massive movement already underway has outflanked all the state's options.

Worker-Student Action Committee, May 21

OPEN LETTER TO SHOP WORKERS, OTHER WAGE EARNERS AND STUDENTS

WE WORKERS IN THE FNAC CHAIN OF SHOPS,

have gone on strike not to see particular demands satisfied, but to take part in the movement which now mobilizes ten million manual and intellectual workers. Through a local agreement reached in April we have already obtained advantages which other workers do not enjoy, and although we support all the demands of the workers and students:

  — wage increase
  — 40 hour week
  — social security
  — free university
  — pensions, etc.

WE DO NOT MAKE THESE OUR FINAL AIMS!

We are taking part in this movement (which is not only about quantitative demands) because ten million workers don't stop work at the same time for a pay rise of F6.30 or 100 centimes, but to challenge the legitimacy of the whole leadership of the country and all the structures of society.

Until the present day, a small minority, the propertied class, has held real power in the country; the Trusts, Monopolies, and Banks make decisions over our whole lives, from the cradle to the grave.

For example, in order to sell their oil they have decided to prioritize the car industry rather than the construction of houses or humanly habitable towns.

They decided the structures, the courses and curricula in the primary and secondary schools, faculties, and universities in order that the technicians, engineers, teachers, and managerial staff should obediently be put at their disposal.

Nobody asked us whether the enormous amount of knowledge and labor which atomic energy demands will be used for the common good or the manufacture of the A or H bomb!

This group, this leadership, this repressive (in all its meanings of the word) power, we challenge in its present form, and in all other variations.

The workers want it replaced by a power that would really and democratically represent them, that's to say by the initiation of self management at workplace, public service, and national level.

Until now nobody has asked the strikers themselves why they are fighting and what they want.

It's necessary that they should be able to express themselves and not only at the local level.

Mass delegations ELECTED BY ALL THE STRIKERS IN EACH WORKPLACE MUST MEET AT THE WORKERS' AND STUDENTS' GENERAL ASSEMBLIES TO DISCUSS THE FUTURE DIRECTION OF THE COUNTRY.

Nobody can arrogate to himself the right to speak in the name of the ten million strikers, to forbid them to speak with the students, to make decisions, or give the order to return to work.

No more leaders elected for life!

For a true workers' democracy!

Text unanimously
adopted by the General Assembly of 24 May 1968
MAKE CONTACT WITH THE FNAC STRIKE COMMITTEE
6 Boulevard de Sebastopol, Paris 4. TURbigo 29-49.

ONCE AGAIN THE REST OF US WORKERS HAVE BEEN FUCKED OVER

What the bosses have conceded to us by way of wage increases, they'll take back from us sooner or later through an increased cost of living.

1 — Negotiation with our exploiters is an illusion.

Once again there's talk of union freedom. Let's give up the traditional marches between Bastille and Republique.

Open struggle against the ruling class is the condition of our emancipation.

2 — If our old guard tried to fuck over the bosses they wouldn't succeed.

The renowned participation that power would accord us is in fact only integration into its system of exploitation. We have fuck all to do with helping them with their profits.

3 — The gutter press on the payroll of the bourgeoisie predict that we'll end up in

the shit.[10] The best cops have been shown up to be among the old guard of the working class.

Too stupid to understand the power of the strike and the occupation of the factories, they've fallen into a monumental *trap*. Nevertheless, it's no longer a question of making them feel afraid, but of ousting them from power.

They are all so very good at selling our labor power. The rank and file is self-conscious enough to take over economic activity under its own control in order to satisfy its basic needs.

It's out of the question to delegate our powers to others as we do so docilely to parliament; instead it's a question of taking over the production process from the workplace. That is the perspective of workers' power over their work

Some postmen

FALSE IDEAS AND FALSE PROBLEMS

Text rejected by the May 30th session
of The Publicity Action Committee at the Sorbonne.

In which unlikely place can we find the publicitaires'[11] honor? Nowhere. Of course, *publicitaires* acknowledge that they are in the service of the consumer society—whereas journalists, sociologists, urban planners don't.

"Publicitaires" create the consumer society?
They don't create it at all. They are its product.

What could "publicitaires" do in a revolutionary society? Who cares. If there are still *publicitaires*, it's because there is still a consumer society (selling something: object, leisure, culture, like an absolute promise of goodness). If there are still *publicitaires*, it's because the revolution has failed.

Are there "publicitaires" on the other side of the iron curtain? A suggestion, in fact, that on that side the revolutions haven't succeeded.

The "publicitaires" have a noble task: spreading information. Any third rate journalist can simply say that five factories produce reasonable quality spaghetti at reasonably fair prices.

The "publicitaires" have a noble task: advertizing. Perhaps it's necessary to have a bunch of very shrewd professionals to find some detail in order to succeed in selling even a car. If things take a revolutionary turn, there won't be a great need for publicitaires in order to know for example that people have a greater need for housing than for cars.

The "publicitaires" have very great influence?
Wrong. The *publicitaires* are a *tertiary* service who produce nothing and have practically no means of action. There are the news readers who in normal times have great influence. But when the printing presses are occupied, it's the workers who have it.

The "publicitaires" must immediately set to work together to conceive a revolutionary society?

Probably a great number of *publicitaires* didn't wait for 30 May 1968 to notice the existence of political or theoretical issues. All of them reached exceedingly different conclusions. They work — or don't work — with various groups. As for the others... if only they'd start to think about the question of what they might do as individuals, rather than as *publicitaires*. But surely they're not alienated to that extent?

In reality, what can a Publicity Action Committee do? Without seeking to split hairs and define itself as a coherent group, it can only gather all the material means of possible communication, and edit appeals corresponding to the greatest common denominator of all the revolutionary parties in formation.

Proposal: From the March 22 Movement, move left.

WE ARE NOTHING, LET US BE EVERYTHING

WE HAVE COME FROM NOTHING TO ARRIVE AT MISERY.

YES

The free gesture, spontaneous organization of the means of production in the hands of the producers, the reality of immediate needs, organization from the heart and self-interested generosity — these represent the fraternal consciousness of what one is working for: the power of the workers' councils.

Theoretical loyalty must find its practical expression: the consciousness of its reality.

SO

To change the conditions of life, to know how to die, to practice free love, to live one's daily life, to hope from despair, is to understand 1905, Kronstadt, Catalonia, Budapest 1956...

ALSO

To destroy power without taking it. To destroy in order to be Other, and oneself.

THIS IS TO LIVE YOUR OWN POETRY.

Freedom, by overthrowing set relationships, finds its moment of construction. So don't say "Excuse me, officer," say, "Drop dead you bastard" which means:

THE INTERNATIONALIZATION OF THE LIVED.

Conscience is the only thing which must not fall into the trap of constructivism. It is for the time being the only street poetry that works. The minimum program is the ACT OF DESTRUCTION: it is the political act par excellence. It has no controls, no rules. The revolution can only be a daily phenomenon if one wants to fight against the fascination of power. The desire to dominate is still the law of the day, the mentality of the freed slave, the vertigo of obeying in order to be obeyed, the mystique of institutions and the religion of order. The extirpation of fascism and the killing of God is achieved through CHAOS.

Our life is at stake and we shall not stop for fear of losing it. The wolves are Lying in wait. Life is short. We are all our own masters or we are nothing. Given this, work will either be a big joke or it will be EVERYTHING.

I love us all.

Long live the power of the workers' councils.

Down with Yugoslavian self-management.

A Yugoslavian Comrade who knows the ropes
"Enragés of all lands, unite!"

GOB ON THE COLLECTION BOX

Comrades,

The rage to live which erupted in the Latin Quarter *burst* into history as one of those great feasts of *joy* which seizes the throat of a world in which the guarantee of not dying of hunger is exchanged for the certainty of *dying of boredom.* The blood of the cops is intoxicating, and precious are the moments when life emerges so intensely from the cover of the *inauthentic*, elegantly to wipe away the humanist slobber. For too long unappeased, our desires, freed at last from the straightjacket of constraints and isolation, treated themselves to a good slice of pleasure. *This is only the beginning*, people say. Once again the political chicanery of the left has reestablished Order better than anyone else. But it's only a partial set-back in the infernal dance which carries within it the preliminary symptoms of disease. In the red dawn of the insurrectionary festivals, the twilight of the old world, East and West, is everywhere flickering in the light of its fires. Tokyo! Berlin! Los Angeles! Prague! Turin! Warsaw! Stockholm! Here and now, the shock really put the shit up the whole load of CGT–PCF–PSU–FGDS–CFTCFO–SNES leaders and other blockheads of the same stamp. At first the reformist rabble spewed up the worst nonsense against the turn to insurrection that was quickly taken up by the student revolt, then did all they could to *appropriate* it, notwithstanding that they had foully strangled it through the mediation of the scheming scum of UNEF, for political ends whose redundant triviality is well-known. The furious mobs who took over the barricades from the bleating flock of the 13th May, seized only the time for a decomposing understanding orchestrated by the vermin who fostered in the naive – too naive – masses the half-belief that another governmental windbag could change something. *They're fucking around with us*! *They're not fucking around for long*!

In the striking seduction of "dialogue" we can recognize the ultimate disguise of repression-recuperation. The stinking breath behind the dripping smile – police-style nastiness which recycles itself: the extended hand holds a truncheon, while yesterday and today's frozen spectacular culture asphyxiates us so much more surely than the CS gas. *Spit on the offering*! Let's spit on the scandalous dialogue and its sordid reforms, some of which could well have the emptiness of being satisfied. It's the stagnant water of the swamps of servility that lies in wait for us, as soon as calm has returned to the soul.

It's also necessary, since an attempt at *direct rank and file democracy* has been elaborated from 13-16 May in the occupied faculties, for us to support and spread as far as possible the anti-bureaucratic agitation, so that it reaches the working class still being hierarchically throttled by the scum of the union big shots. The activist minorities, cells of lucid resistance from within key sectors, must engage in a permanent *guerrilla harassment* against power; a combined strategy negatively to recover the essential configuration of the system to be destroyed − a grandiose way of sucking the marrow from it which will weaken it as it strengthens us. Given up to the pitiless game of subversion, the social machine overflows with thrilling resources to be exploited. Sabotage, forgery, detournements, frauds, boycotts... which *jubilant creativity* has given itself free rein − a demoniacal storm of illicit pleasures − and many will be the tastes or talents revealed there! Everything will finish well one day by getting back onto the streets.

Furious, healthy wildcat strikes when they happen will have to recognize themselves in their most *ethereal crystalization*. As good as a paving stone in a cop's face, murder in the last resort will *blossom out to the borders of a sublime efficacy*. As for looting and other fine initiatives, to go further they must be seen as the highest achievements of our struggle towards the effective bypassing of the world of the market and reified social relations. In front of shop windows − deforming mirrors where our human image is lost, hardened by money − our regard has too often recognized things and their price. Let's put an end to it! It's only through such a praxis that the reborn revolutionary forces will reach a clear understanding of their struggle. No better way to scrape away the ideological mold!

Although it's such a long time since radical contestation has ridden the ossified old horse of the old bureaucratic leftists − look how their farcical lies compete in the swamps of the *petty bosses* of the groups, whether Trotskyist (JCR, FER, VO), Maoist (UJC, MLF, CV rank and file) or anarchists à la Cohn Bendit. *Let's settle our own affairs ourselves!*

Under the thumb of worm-eaten leaders, unity will only ever mean submission. The revolutionary project must become effectively what it already was essentially, and its clear global coherence to these successive realizations like the immanence of all to the parties. Let's beware! Whatever is lost through partial contestation rejoins the oppressive function of the old world. Senile blunder that is the criticism of the bourgeois university alone is a laugh without relating it to the whole of that class society which must be suppressed − (that's to say dialectically superceded through generalized self-management) − even at its core: the vile and vast human prostitution of alienated labor. Death to waged work! Death to survival! Already can't you hear the distant cry of the hunt? Hunted down Old World, you're at your last gasp. You're for the chop old bastard!

Long live the Zengakuren (Japan)!
Long live the Vandalist Committee of Public Safety (Bordeaux)!
Long live the Enragés (Nanterre)!
Long live the Situationist International!
Long live the revolution of daily life!

The Montgeron Enragés

ANNOUNCEMENT

We are pleased to inform you of the steps that will be taken the day that the police invade OUR faculty.

Complete and utter destruction of the greatest amount of machinery, furniture, windows, lights, offices... It's quite obvious that fires will be inevitable.

THE ODEON, THE SORBONNE, THE FINE ART DEPARTMENT, have shown us the direction not to be followed.

With or without the Enragés, CENSIER will be STALINGRAD, NEWARK, WARSAW, KHE SAHN, but WILL NOT BE a new step backwards, with our pants round our ankles.

"Workers–Students don't let yourselves be fucked over" Committee!

Notes

[1] A "new town" development north of Paris.

[2] On the back of the leaflet was a reproduction of the painting of the same name by Marcel Duchamp. This is a very difficult piece to translate and understand; it shows up the relative obscurity of reference and terminology of some of the Enragés tracts. It would, however, bring a wry smile to anyone "in the know."

[3] Leftist sociologist who plagiarized situationist writings.

[4] Leftist journal boycotted by the situationists from 1960 for its conformism and pseudo-intellectualism. It persistently ignored the situationists, whilst printing Lefebvre's plagiarisms.

[5] Militant Japanese group, believed by the S.I. to be politically close to them.

[6] National Center for Scientific Research.

[7] Title of an old song from the Commune of 1871.

[8] Director of Nanterre.

[9] National Young Doctors' Center.

[10] Loose translation of "chienlit," archaic barrackroom slang used by de Gaulle about the state the country was in, meaning literally, "dog's bed" — akin to the English expression "dog's breakfast." "Reforms yes, but no dog's breakfast."

[11] The French term "publicitaire" covers people in advertising, PR and publicity work in general. Here it also implies that such people are "self-publicists."

"TO BE CONTINUED..."